Scenarios for Teaching Writing

College Section Committee

/ ૪ ૭ ૦

Scenarios for Teaching Writing

Contexts for Discussion and Reflective Practice

Chris M. Anson
University of Minnesota

Joan Graham
University of Washington

David A. Jolliffe
University of Illinois at Chicago

Nancy S. Shapiro
University of Maryland at College Park

Carolyn H. Smith
University of Florida

Published by
National Council of Teachers of English
1111 W. Kenyon Road, Urbana, Illinois 61801-1096
in cooperation with
Alliance for Undergraduate Education
405 Old Main, University Park, Pennsylvania 16802

NCTE Stock Number 42559-3050

The Alliance for Undergraduate Education is a cooperative project of major public research universities aimed at improving the quality of undergraduate education. Members of the Alliance are The University of Arizona; the University of California, Berkeley; the University of California, Los Angeles; the University of Florida; The University of Illinois; Indiana University; The University of Maryland at College Park; The University of Michigan; the University of Minnesota; the University of North Carolina–Chapel Hill; The Ohio State University; The Pennsylvania State University; Rutgers, The State University of New Jersey; The University of Texas at Austin; the University of Washington; and the University of Wisconsin–Madison.

Library of Congress Cataloging-in-Publication Data

Scenarios for teaching writing : contexts for discussion and reflective practice / Chris M. Anson . . . [et al.].
   p. cm.
   Includes bibliographical references (p.).
   "NCTE stock number 42559-3050"—T.p. verso.
   ISBN 0-8141-4255-9 : $16.95
   1. English language—Rhetoric—Study and teaching.
I. Anson, Christopher M., 1954–
PE1404.S33   1993
808'.042071'173—dc20   92-47414
                                                                   CIP

Contents

Acknowledgments

Our first debt of gratitude must go to the many teachers, most of them graduate students at our respective universities, who generously provided the contexts, papers, syllabi, and experiences described in this book. As we reflected, while drafting the manuscript, on the ways we are drawn into the interesting situations of these teachers, we began to appreciate how our positions as administrators of large writing programs continually compel us to make our practice more reflective and intellectually challenging. To these teachers we are grateful not just for giving us some of the grist for this book, but for many hours of interesting and educative discussion.

We wish to acknowledge the generous support of the Alliance for Undergraduate Education, whose Board of Governors took an immediate interest in this project and saw to it that we could meet for several long weekends in Chicago and Minneapolis to draft and revise the manuscript. Anne Nelson, executive director of the Alliance, deserves our special thanks for her encouragement and attention to the administrative details of our sponsorship. We also thank the administrations of our own institutions—the universities of Florida, Illinois at Chicago, Maryland, Minnesota, and Washington—for supporting the development of the manuscript and for funding our appearance at the annual meetings of the Alliance Writing Group.

Carrie Brecke undertook the difficult task of assembling the initial manuscript and deciphering our numerous line-by-line revisions, and we are grateful to her for her patience and good will. We are also grateful to the many colleagues (especially Dennis Baron of the University of Illinois at Urbana–Champaign), graduate students, and others who read all or part of the manuscript and gave us useful feedback.

The order of authorship is purely alphabetical. Late in the project, as we looked back over our two years of drafting and redrafting and revising, we all agreed that the manuscript represents the most collaborative effort any of us has ever experienced as a writer. Hardly a paragraph exists which does not bear the mark of each of our hands (or, as was more often the case, all of our hands at once).

Introduction

Current and prospective teachers of introductory university writing courses face many challenges. Students come to our courses with widely differing academic abilities and experiences. Often they are just learning to deal with a new level of academic challenge—more difficult subject matter, more reading and homework, stiffer competition. At the same time, they face new kinds of personal challenges—financing their education, living independently, and finding their own intellectual, moral, spiritual, and sexual identities. It is this demanding audience we must teach, interacting with them daily, adjusting our instruction to their development, and teaching the bodies of knowledge and the ways of thinking, writing, and speaking that prevail in the field. It's a tough job.

It's made even tougher by the fact that many teachers of writing, especially those just beginning their careers, have not had much opportunity to think carefully about a variety of challenging instructional issues. If you are a new teaching assistant pursuing a master's or doctoral degree and supporting yourself by teaching, your time to devote to teaching may be constrained by the rigors of graduate studies, financial pressures, or commitments to family. If you are a new faculty member, you must balance the demands of tenure-driven research and publication with time-consuming efforts to teach effectively. If you are a part-time, temporary, or adjunct instructor, resources for professional development may be few, and because of other professional and personal commitments, you may be unable to take full advantage of those resources that are available. And, if you are an experienced teacher but have not recently taught composition, you may feel the need to rethink some of your methods or beliefs in the wide wake of new scholarship and teaching practices in the field of composition studies.

College composition has become a huge industry. Almost 90 percent of all first-year students must take some type of writing course, amounting to more than $50 million of instruction in the United States each year. Accompanying this enormous enterprise is a bewildering array of curricular designs, teaching methods, philosophies, and resources (especially the more than $40 million of college composition textbooks sold each year, a market which represents every conceivable approach to writing instruction). Teaching effectively means sorting through these often conflicting ideas and making principled decisions about course design, curricular materials, and pedagogical methods.

This book assumes that experience can be wise counsel. Examining the experiences of others can help all instructors to become familiar with key issues in the teaching of writing, introducing them, in practical terms, to composition as a field of study and to the art of teaching as constantly renewed inquiry. The book was written by the Working Group on Writing Instruction and Assessment of the Alliance for Undergraduate Education, a consortium of sixteen large, research-oriented state universities: Arizona; California, Berkeley; California, Los Angeles; Florida; Illinois; Indiana; Maryland at College Park; Michigan; Minnesota; North Carolina–Chapel Hill; Ohio State; Pennsylvania State; Rutgers; Texas at Austin; Washington; and Wisconsin–Madison. Since 1985, members of this working group, all faculty involved with undergraduate writing programs at their respective institutions, have met twice yearly to discuss ways to improve writing instruction and to encourage the use of writing as a tool for learning, thinking, and communicating throughout the curriculum.

Scenarios for Teaching Writing offers six chapters of "real-world" scenarios about different aspects of teaching writing, each containing issues for discussion. Chapter 1 focuses on one of the most fundamental tasks of the writing instructor: designing principled, effective, engaging writing assignments for students. Chapter 2 focuses on the uses of readings in writing courses. Chapter 3 examines principles, methods, and problems of responding to student writing. Chapter 4 considers the complicated aspects of teaching grammar, usage, and style in a writing course. Chapter 5 deals with issues of managing discourse, the teacher's role in the writing classroom, and teacher-student interaction. Chapter 6 takes a global perspective on writing courses by presenting several quite different course designs that represent diverse assumptions about the goals, methods, and teaching practices in writing courses.

The names of students and teachers in the scenarios are fictitious and, in some cases, the situations have been slightly modified or elaborated; however, *the substance of each scenario is real and current.* As authors of this book—experienced administrators of university writing programs and preparers of new teachers—we have assembled these scenarios from actual events that occurred in our own writing programs. Most of the events took place over the past two or three years in the classrooms and offices of new instructors who consulted us for advice. The sample syllabi, assignments, papers, journal entries, and transcripts of group conferences are *all real.* We have included those situations that seemed the most important for writing teachers to reflect upon and those that present the most engaging theoretical and practical puzzles for discussion.

Suggestions for Using This Book

The scenarios and discussion questions can be used in at least two types of settings. First, they are ideally suited for use in introductory graduate seminars or training workshops on teaching writing, such as those required for new teaching assistants at large universities. These seminars now use an increasing number of excellent books on composition theory and pedagogy. *Scenarios for Teaching Writing* is intended to bring to life, in realistic settings, the theoretical issues and varied approaches characteristic of current inquiry in the field. Second, the scenarios may be used as discussion prompts for writing teachers who meet informally but regularly to discuss their teaching. Participants can discuss one scenario to begin a meeting and then move on to discuss related experiences in their own teaching.

In such settings, instructors might read one or more scenarios independently and write short responses to them. These responses can then become the basis either for small-group or large-group discussion, depending on the size of the seminar or workshop. Discussions might focus first on the diversity of opinion emerging from the individual critiques, and then move toward establishing consensus within the general philosophies and policies of a given writing program. Graduate courses can, of course, turn written and group responses into assignments to be revised and submitted as required course work.

Finally, we envision that *Scenarios for Teaching Writing* might be used productively among even the most seasoned of writing teachers in an effort to increase dialogue and encourage more reflective practice. In workshops where we have used some of the scenarios among highly experienced teachers, the discussions were nothing short of dynamic. Good teachers, like good writers, are often the most eager to confess their tentativeness, constantly experimenting with new ideas and methods as they themselves develop and change throughout their careers. The scenarios published here are designed, in part, to help keep their dialogue going.

It is important to realize that these scenarios *do not necessarily mirror every aspect of the program in which they might be used.* However, their underlying themes—themes of interpersonal conflict, gender identity, role, power, ownership, purpose, and the aims of higher literacy—cut across institutional boundaries to affect all of us, inexperienced teaching assistants or seasoned professors, in ways that bear directly on how we grow and change as teachers of writing.

In this sense, you might use the scenarios to raise general questions about a range of instructional issues that you can then particularize in your own classes. Either during or after your discussions of the scenarios, you can turn your attention to the ongoing pedagogical concerns in your own courses and program. You and your colleagues might also consider writing your own scenarios, contextualized in the more specific setting where you teach, and sharing these with other teachers at your institution.

You should not feel compelled to consider the scenarios in order. The chapters move, as a seminar might, from general issues of assignment design and the selection of material to more particular concerns of interacting with students, then finally to the broad consideration of course design as a whole; but each scenario forms an independent unit.

You will notice that these scenarios offer neither solutions nor models for imitation. The omission is, of course, deliberate. Experienced teachers of introductory courses attest time and again that they learn how to cope with problems like those presented here by meeting them head on. As authors of this collection, we might have said, "Oh, here's what we would do at Minnesota" (or Washington or Maryland or Florida or Illinois at Chicago), but we believe that sample problems, like actual problems, should be solved in dialogue among teachers at particular institutions. Thus, while the questions we offer for discussion may suggest our biases toward the issues we think are at stake in each scenario, we have deliberately avoided closing down inquiry and discussion by advocating our own interpretations or solutions.

In a number of scenarios, we have alluded to (or actually cited) specific textbooks, methods, and materials currently available to new instructors. In none of these cases should our allusions to these materials be considered either an endorsement or a criticism. One of the principal ideas underlying this book is that new instructors themselves should become familiar with what is available for them to work with and gain the experience and the expertise to judge wisely for themselves what they want to use.

You will also notice the conspicuous absence of professional readings on composition theory, practice, and research. Such readings might provide expert opinion possibly useful for interpreting and solving the problems raised in the scenarios. However, a selection of readings might also suggest *definitive* solutions, which runs against our theory that teaching, like writing, is interpretive, interpersonal, and contextual. Instead, each author "nominated" a dozen readings on the issues raised in each chapter, from which we selected the top choices and included them in a short bibliography at the end of the book. In courses or training programs, these might become the start of a useful archive of information on the teaching of writing.

We have consciously decided to keep the focus of this book on the pragmatic needs of writing instructors. Consequently, in our brief introductions to each chapter, we have mentioned almost no theoretical works or research reports. Of course, we do not mean to suggest that scholarship in composition has little to offer teachers, who need only learn the local lore about writing instruction at their institution. Instead, we see this collection of scenarios as just one invitation to inquire into the complexities and theoretical richness of college-level writing instruction.

1 Creating Effective Writing Assignments

When we think of designing a writing course, we think primarily of how we will engage our students in meaningful writing projects. Of all the clichés in the business, "Students learn to write by writing" stands out as one of the oldest and truest. What we tell students (lectures) and what we have them read may prepare them for writing, but only *by* writing do they become more competent and mature as writers. What will we have them write? Does it matter how we extend "assisted invitations" to write? Does it matter how we order our assignments— which ones we start with, which ones come later? And if those things matter, are there any guidelines that help us generate engaging, interesting writing assignments?

This chapter presents scenarios drawn from the experiences of typical college writing teachers. The first scenario, a set of three brief case studies, deals with what we might call the microlevel of assignment making: What does a good individual assignment sheet look like? What type of genre or written output should you look for? The second scenario addresses a pedagogical issue: What should you do when your expectations as a teacher do not match the reality of your class? The third scenario presents a number of assignment ideas, but asks a more global question: How would you sequence these assignments? What principles of learning or cognitive development might help guide a sequence? What are the "cognitive aims" of different assignments— are some more complex than others? Can we apply any hierarchies to assignment sequencing? And the fourth scenario tests our limits for what counts as an "appropriate" response to a writing assignment.

Articulating Writing Assignments: The Peer Teacher Team

Brian Jackson, Margo Brown, and Linda Barton are three writing instructors at a large university. Brian and Margo are first-year teaching assistants (TAs), and Linda has been around the English department for several years as a graduate student. Because of their similar teaching schedules, these three have been assigned to the same peer teacher team (one of the support structures the university sets up for instructors). The team members are expected to meet regularly to discuss their writing and reading assignments, student papers, and any other issues or topics that grow out of their teaching experiences.

Early in the semester they settle into a routine where each one takes a turn presenting a draft of an assignment at successive weekly meetings. The group critiques an assignment, and then the author revises it on the basis of insights gained from the group's discussion.

As you read through these case studies, you will come to see how teachers in the same program can approach similar types of assignments with different theoretical assumptions and different expectations of their students. As you work through the questions developed around the individual assignments, do not hesitate to move between and among the three, comparing and contrasting the language, style, focus, and purposes of the assignments.

For the purposes of this discussion, you can assume that when the teachers refer to a common text (for example, Freire), they engaged the class in some related discussion and informal prewriting leading up to these assignment sheets.

Bring It Back: A Narrative Assignment

Brian Jackson came to graduate school after teaching for three years in a high school and working part-time at a local newspaper. He was more mature than most of the new graduate students and had some practical teaching experience to draw on as he faced his first introductory freshman writing class. Yet, while his high school teaching experience may have given him more "presence" in the classroom those first few weeks, he felt quite unprepared to create the type of writing assignments that had been introduced in his new-TA orientation.

Brian was used to giving assignments drawn from readings in a required American literature high school textbook, the kind that asked students to analyze characters, identify themes, and relate one work to another. But throughout his weeklong TA orientation, the directors of the writing program emphasized writing in an academic context. They spoke of freshmen joining the "academic discourse community" (whatever that meant). During orientation, Brian learned that writing assignments should be designed to encourage "critical thinking and reflection at the college level." The directors identified three elements of a successful college writing assignment:

1. Specify the content.
2. Suggest or identify some prewriting stimuli.

3. Give the assignment some rhetorical context—that is, give the students an audience and purpose to write for.

After a week and a half of classes, Brian tried conscientiously to follow his directors in setting up his first writing assignment. Brian's assignment appears below.

Narrative Assignment

Narratives tell stories. In this assignment you will tell the story of a significant educational experience you have had. What is a "significant educational experience," you ask? Any event which enlarges or alters your thinking could be considered an educational experience.

In a recent interview with <u>Omni</u> magazine, Paulo Freire, whom you've all read, relates a "significant educational experience" he had as a young boy. He explains the influence of his mother on his early education: "I had been taught by my mother, a woman with the rigid ethics of a devout Catholic." Then he relays this autobiographical story:

> One day my brothers and I caught a neighbor's chicken that had wandered into our yard. We killed it. My mother heard the chicken's cries and came running. I expected her to punish us, give the chicken back to the neighbor, and ask him to forgive us. But she picked it up, went to the kitchen, and we ate it. A beautiful lunch! She was very realistic. I forgot the incident until much later, after she died. But I've often wondered what sort of turmoil she went through as she stood there looking at the dead chicken, then at us, deciding if she should return it or feed us. (pp. 74, 78-79, 94)

Imagine the young boy's shock at his devout Catholic mother's behavior. Stealing is a sin, but they were starving, and a mother has an obligation to her children . . .

Before slaying the chicken, the eleven-year-old Freire saw the world, and perhaps particularly his mother, as two-dimensional, black and white, right and wrong. However, after his mother's reaction, he begins to see that life is not as simple as an immature Catholic perspective may want to frame it.

If Freire were writing this assignment, he would emphasize a particular aspect of this day in his telling of the story. For example, he may want to emphasize his surprise and bewilderment regarding his mother's reaction. Or he may wish to emphasize how he really feared his mother, but feared his brothers more, and therefore went along with something he thought they would be punished for.

Whichever aspect he chooses to describe, however, would not be the point of the narrative. <u>The reason for writing the story is to tell how he learned from the event.</u> The emphasized aspect dramatizes the educational process as it occurs and brings the narrative to life. For us to see how Freire learned from the experience, though, we need to know how he thought before the incident, and how he thinks afterwards. Be sure to include such information in your own narratives.

    Remember: Write your name and any other pertinent information (i.e., the date, the class) in the upper right corner of the first page; center the title, and put one staple through the upper left corner of the pages. You may want to put your last name alongside the page numbers of pages 2, 3, etc. The narrative is due at the beginning of class on Wednesday, October 3.

ISSUES FOR DISCUSSION

• If you were a student in Brian's class, what would you think of this as the first assignment? Can you think of an incident that you would write about? Is there anything in this assignment that could help a student decide on a topic? Was the Freire anecdote helpful?

• To what extent does the assignment encourage college-level critical thinking? To what extent does the assignment reflect the three elements of a successful writing assignment outlined above?

• Brian offers this written rationale for his first writing assignment in the course:

> I'm assigning such an essay at the start of the semester, and thus at the start of my students' college experience (they are all first-year frosh, seventeen to eighteen years old), with the goal of getting them to be more self-conscious of their education. I think many students come to college with the high school schedule and routine still well entrenched in their minds. Time outside of class becomes "free" time in which you don't talk about "school." I hope that this assignment may begin to break down some of those mental corridors established by high school modular scheduling. I am curious to see how many of them will write of events that happened outside of school, which they later saw as significant because of some discussion or activity in school. Then, perhaps, they could see how "school" is related to the "real world." The goal is to have the students rethink how events that stand out in their memory because of their significance may be formidable educational experiences.

What do you think of Brian's rationale?

• Margo read Brian's assignment and just shook her head. "Come on, Brian!" she chided. "You know that when you ask them to write about what they learned from some experience, you'll just get that trite garbage, like 'I learned a lot' or 'I really grew up.' You've got to do better than that if you want anything original." Do you agree with Margo?

• Linda had a different objection. "These kids aren't ready for Freire—haven't you figured that out yet? You've got to teach them to walk before they can run. If you ask them to do too much—like where you ask them to reflect on 'how they learned from an event, how they think about it differently before and afterwards'—I bet you won't even get a decent narrative, let alone a thoughtful essay." What do you think of Linda's comments?

• Would you use this assignment or an assignment like it?

Fight It Out: An Argumentative Assignment

Unlike Brian, Margo Brown has no prior classroom experience. A new twenty-two-year-old graduate student working for a master's degree in fine arts (creative writing), she worries about presenting herself as confident and knowledgeable about composition. As a poet, she intuitively speaks and writes in metaphors, and her images are often quite striking. She wants her students to come to appreciate the beauty and power of language, but she clearly understands that the freshman writing class is not the place to offer creative writing instruction. She is committed to helping her students excel in the academy by learning effective strategies for academic writing.

In presenting her second assignment to her peer team, she was quick to point out how her ideas about getting students to think about academic writing differed from Brian's. Her argumentative assignment follows.

The Argument Paper

We have been studying strategies that different writers use when they write argumentative essays. For this assignment, you will be taking a position on a controversial topic and applying the strategies that we have discussed. Today's newspapers are filled with hotly debated issues: Should condoms be distributed in high schools? Should euthanasia be legal? Should mass murderers be able to plead temporary insanity? Should addictive drugs be legalized? Should health care workers be tested for AIDS? Obviously, you can think of many more.

As you plan your position paper, imagine an audience that holds the diametrically opposite viewpoint. To argue forcefully, you must marshal your facts, organize them strategically in a way that outmaneuvers your opponent, and anticipate the potential objections from your readers. The more ammunition you have in the way of facts and rhetorical strategies, the more effective you will be. If you can find out your opponent's positions and usual lines of argument, you will be in a position to discredit and shoot down these objections before they can be raised.

Your weapons include definition, analogy, example, comparison and contrast—in fact, all the rhetorical strategies we have been discussing in class. Imagine that the context for your argument is a letter to the editor of the college newspaper or your local, hometown newspaper. You begin with credibility as a member of the community you are addressing. Remember that your purpose is to destroy the advocates of the other position with the logic of your own position. You are not required to do research for this paper, but you may want to arm yourself with a few facts from reliable sources.

Due: Oct. 14

Length: 3-5 pages

ISSUES FOR DISCUSSION

- Is this an appropriate early assignment for a freshman writing class?

- What topics would you expect students to write about for this paper? Where should they go for information?

- How well do you think Margo addressed all three necessary aspects of the assignment: content, stimuli, and rhetorical situation?

- When asked about her rationale, Margo wrote:

> The purpose of this assignment was to get my students to flex their rhetorical muscles. I realize that argument is one of the more difficult rhetorical modes, but I also think it is the most stimulating. I want my students to write because they care deeply about something. I believe that the best writing comes from that emotional involvement. The more they practice integrating the rhetorical strategies in their writing, the more fluent they will become.
>
> I try to emphasize that writing is not merely a record of events or a transcription of thoughts—instead, it constitutes an epistemological process that would be non-existent without the written word. I address the idea of audience by giving them concrete situations that they could actually imagine themselves in.

- Brian liked the rhetorical context that Margo provided for this assignment, but he was worried. "Aren't you afraid that your students will just fill up pages with rant?" he asked.

"Is that so bad?" Margo wanted to know. "At least they'll be practicing rhetoric." Do you agree with Margo or Brian? Why?

- Linda liked Margo's assignment a lot, too. "My only concern is that you don't tell them how to do this," she offered. "Don't you leave yourself open to lots of questions about sources and topics and things like that? Do you think they'll take your suggestions as the best ideas?" Do you agree with Linda?

● Would you use this assignment or an assignment like it? Why or why not?

Look It Up: A Research Paper Assignment

At the other end of the spectrum from Brian and Margo is Linda Barton, an advanced graduate student who is in the last stages of writing her dissertation and spends a lot of time in the library. Because her fellowship has expired, she petitioned to teach a section of freshman writing as an instructor. She also teaches part-time at a local community college. As she plans her courses, Linda recalls her previous teachers who emphasized library research as a tool for succeeding in college. She wants to equip her students with those same kinds of skills. The research paper assignment reprinted below came toward the end of her course.

The Research Paper: Assignment Sheet

Due: Dec. 7

Length: 3-4 typed pages

First. Decide on a topic. (We'll do some brainstorming in class—you can also locate some worthwhile political topics by reading the newspaper.) Be sure to try to pick a topic you're interested in.

Second. Go to the campus library and find the New York Times and Washington Post indexes. Find your topic in the indexes and read their summaries of the articles' contents. Write down any titles, dates, etc. of the ones that look as if they'd have information that would help in your research, either those that seem to specifically relate to your topic, those that may have good detailed information, or those that would provide helpful background information you (as an expert) would need to know in order to write authoritatively. Find the microfilm of the New York Times and the Washington Post; then find and read the articles you're looking for. Take notes as you read. Perhaps photocopy some of the more important articles. **Be sure to record all bibliographic information.**

Third. Go to the Reader's Guide and see if any magazine articles were written on your subject. Find a few by (first) finding out if the university (or your local library) owns issues of that magazine, and (second) find its location in the library (one of several possible places). (At any point in this [some-

times frustrating] process you start to go crazy, ask the librar-
ians for help—that's what they're there for.) Read some of the
articles, take notes, possibly photocopy a few articles.

Next. Continue to fill in gaps, and begin to write. What I am
looking for is an essay, that is, paragraphs that are unified,
filled with facts (quotes, statistics, incidents, examples, details,
names, etc.) that support their paragraph's clear, well thought
out topic sentence. In turn, each paragraph's topic sentence
should address the paper's thesis—and the thesis will itself
be the answer to the question asked either by you or chosen
by you from those on the "Suggested Research Topics"
page. **Remember: This paper must have a thesis.**

Finally. Finish your research. Write your paper. Revise it as
much as it needs in order to be clear, tight, convincing, and
obviously the best paper you've written in here so far. Proof it
carefully. Make sure your paper's documentation is clear and
accurate. **Plagiarism is serious—whether intentional or not.**

* DO NOT use articles or sources more than three years old.
* DO NOT wait until the last minute to begin your library
  research.
* All papers must be typed, double-spaced, with 1-inch mar-
  gins on all sides.
* Use MLA style for citations and works cited.

ISSUES FOR DISCUSSION

• How would you respond to this assignment if you were one of
Linda's students?

• How well has Linda incorporated the three essentials (content,
stimuli, and rhetorical context) in her assignment?

• What kind of papers do you expect that Linda will receive on the
basis of these instructions?

• At this point in the peer-group discussions, Brian begins to express
doubts about the purpose of assignments. "I'm worried that my first
assignment was so wishy-washy," he commented. "Linda's looks so
much more straightforward and easier to follow."

Margo, on the other hand, expressed veiled contempt for Linda's
assignment: "It looks like a cookbook variety assignment," she muttered.
"Anybody could teach writing if this is all you have to do." How do
you react to Brian's and Margo's comments?

• Linda reflects on her assignment:

    I believe that writing assignments should offer students as
    much concrete support as possible. In this assignment I really
    did not concern myself too much with the topic of their pa-

per—it was the process that I was especially interested in. I think students appreciate explicit directions—exactly what to do, and what <u>not</u> to do should be spelled out. That way, students won't have to guess what the teacher wants. I constructed this assignment to be free from the diversionary, mysterious chitchat that I've seen in some assignments.

What do you think of Linda's rationale?

• Would you use this assignment or one like it? Why or why not?

• Look at the differences in tone among the three assignment sheets. What effect do you think tone will have on the students' responses to these assignments?

• Which tone do you like most of the three? Why?

Todd's Assignment Backfires

Todd Froelich was teaching his first section of basic English, a course designed for inexperienced student writers who need to prepare for the university's general introductory writing course. Todd had taught the general introductory course four times, and he had enjoyed having students read professional texts about contemporary social and political issues, discuss the issues in class, and then write essays in response to rather open-ended prompts. He found that the students really became engaged in discussing topics like race, gender roles, environmental ethics, and the like. Moreover, after considerable experimentation with the wording of writing assignments, he determined that the students actually wrote much better if the assignment did not guide them too much—if it did not prescribe exactly who the audience of their text was supposed to be, what its primary purpose was, what format the essay should take, how long it should be, and so on. As the students wrote their essays and conferred with Todd and their peers about drafts, these issues would get fleshed out in discussion.

While preparing his first major assignment for basic English, Todd assumed that the same strategy would work well with the inexperienced student writers. If anything, he thought, these students might be even more comfortable, and therefore more successful, if he were not too directive—if he did not seem to be taking too much initiative for making decisions about audience, purpose, genre, stance, and so on away from the students. They need to succeed as writers, Todd thought, and this leeway will allow them to do so.

His plan for the first week of class, containing three sessions, was fairly straightforward. On the first day, as usual, he would introduce policies and principles and go over the syllabus. He assigned the students to read a brief, humorous piece, "I Want a Wife," by Judy Syfers, for the next session. They spent the hour discussing the main idea of the essay, the structure and diction, and the character of the speaker. At the end of class that day, Todd handed out the following writing assignment:

> If you feel that traditional gender roles are disappearing from present-day society, discuss those influences that are responsible for weakening them.

He told the students to work on a draft of an essay responding to this assignment and to bring their drafts to class for the final session of week one. At that session, Todd explained, the students would trade papers with a classmate and discuss ways to revise their drafts into more polished essays.

At the next class session, much to Todd's surprise, only four of the fifteen students had written any kind of draft in response to the assignment. Three others had written down a few notes about the topic, but nothing they could share with a peer reader. Eight of the fifteen came to class empty-handed.

Todd was flabbergasted. "Why didn't you write anything?" he asked, trying to keep his cool. Nobody said a word. "Okay," he said, "let's write your questions about this assignment on the board and talk about them." Finally, one student spoke up: "Were we supposed to use the story we read for class when we wrote this theme?" Once the ice was broken, two other students raised their hands quickly. "What's an influence?" one young woman asked. "How do we discuss something in an essay?" a young man blurted out. "Don't you have to have at least two people to have a discussion? And there's only one person writing an essay, right?"

Todd realized that he needed to rethink his pedagogical approach.

ISSUES FOR DISCUSSION

• How should Todd respond to each of the questions the students put to him on the last day of the first week's classes?

• For different kinds of students—basic, general, or honors students—how much guidance should a writing assignment provide about the following features:

> The need to conduct research?
>
> The potential use of readings?
>
> The intellectual tasks called for?

The genre?

The length?

The audience?

The purpose?

Any other features?

A Sequence of Dilemmas

Greg Holsebach, a first-year teaching assistant who was planning his freshman writing syllabus, was very concerned about offering his students good writing assignments. As part of his planning, he talked to several experienced teachers and asked them to provide model or sample assignments. He was so impressed by several of them that he decided the best way to structure his own course was to ask his students to write essays based on five of the best assignments he collected. His problem, though, was that he was not sure how to sequence the assignments in a way that would work to increase his students' competence little by little. He was afraid of overwhelming the students with too many cognitive demands, inadvertently exacerbating the writer's block of already anxious freshmen.

Greg identified five related cognitive aims—goals he hoped the students would achieve through writing activities in the course:

1. Appreciate what they already know about a subject.
2. Discover new knowledge and new ways of thinking about a subject.
3. Reflect on their changing ideas.
4. Anticipate and accommodate readers' needs.
5. Take a critical perspective on their own writing.

Greg knew that it is a lot easier to list goals or objectives for a course than it is to accomplish them in a term, but he felt that if he were careful about sequencing his assignments and provided enough support at each level, students would be able to use these strategies to continue to improve their thinking and writing throughout their undergraduate careers.

After considerable deliberation, Greg decided on a sequence for the five major assignments in his course. To solicit one more reaction to his plan, he showed the assignments, in the sequence he intended to give them, to Louise Roth, his faculty adviser. Here are the five assignments in the order Greg intended to give them:

Assignments[1]

1. After reading Alfred Kazin's essay "The Kitchen," think about the kitchen you grew up in. Can you recall details that led to a dominant impression? Quite possibly many of the individual memories clash—you will remember both happy and sad times, bustling activity and quiet times. Begin by searching your memory for many details of the kitchen, including people and events associated with that space. Then try to distill a single impression, and select from your long list those elements that would recreate the impression for a reader.

2. Watch two episodes of a popular TV series ("Cosby," "Roseanne," "Family Ties," etc.) and take notes on the depiction of social class on TV. You may pay attention to living conditions, jobs, speech patterns, possessions, leisure activities, etc. Hint: you might want to think about what is not included in the show (are poor people represented? people from different cultures?). What assumptions are being made by the producers? Write a critique for your local newspaper about how social class is portrayed on television.

3. Write an extended definition of a significant term from your major or from an area that you know reasonably well. Your audience is the general public, and your purpose is to clarify the meaning of a term your audience may not have heard of or may have misconceptions about.

4. Read the Time magazine article on "The Simple Life: Rejecting the Rat Race, Americans Get Back to Basics" (April 8, 1991, pp. 58–63). First, write a summary of the article, identifying the main points of the argument. What is the author trying to demonstrate or prove? What kind of evidence does the author use? Second, interview three people (preferably of different generations or different backgrounds) about their reactions to the thesis presented by this article. You can summarize it for them briefly, then ask if they agree with the thesis. Third, referring to the original article and the notes you took from your interviews, formulate your own analysis of this thesis. Does a trend really exist, or is the author or editor forcing the issue? Write your response as a letter to the editor of Time.

5. After reading two opposing articles on affirmative action (one pro and one con), ask students to write a letter to the editor of the college newspaper, supporting or criticizing the current affirmative action policies of their university.

The next day after showing his mentor the assignments in his proposed sequence, Greg found this note from her in his mailbox:

Greg:

Your assignments all look interesting as isolated exercises, but for the life of me, I can't see what principle underlines them so that collectively they could constitute a legitimate writing course. What reason do students have for proceeding from one assignment to the next? What kinds of inquiry are they going to be engaging in for the entire term? How will that inquiry develop? How will your assignments support the process of inquiry? Here's a suggestion: Rather than having students write in response to all five of these assignments, why not select just one and really ask students to "unpack" it in several smaller assignments. For example, you could break up the assignment, using the series of questions James Moffett sets out in Teaching the Universe of Discourse: *What is happening? (Drama) What happened? (Narration) What happens? (Generalization) What might happen if? (Argument). Or you could develop a sequence of assignments based on James Kinneavy's major aims, explained in* A Theory of Discourse: *expressive writing, referential writing (informative, exploratory, and demonstrative), and persuasive writing. You could even adopt some form of the "modes" or methods of exposition: description, narration, definition, comparison, classification, and so on. If the assignments are so subdivided, your students could work very hard on one—or maybe two—of them during the course. I think you'll find that the students will learn a lot more both about how to write effectively and about how writing fosters learning. I'd be happy to discuss your syllabus in greater detail at your convenience.*

Best,

Louise

ISSUES FOR DISCUSSION

● What do you think of Greg's initial plan to ask his colleagues to give him successful sample or model writing assignments from their classes? What are the benefits and the problems in this practice?

● What do you think about the advice Louise Roth offers Greg? What suggestions would you give him as he plans his syllabus? How would you explain your rationale for sequencing?

● If you were to use any of the five assignments Greg chose, would you want to modify them in terms of audience, purpose, or complexity?

Personal Porn

Chris Eastman has been teaching composition as a part-time (adjunct) faculty member at a large university for almost six years. His teaching method includes peer-revision conferences, which take place each time his students have written a full rough draft of an assignment. During the week of conferences, Chris cancels two regular class sessions and meets, one at a time, with each group of four students, usually in the cafeteria of the university student union. His conference style is facilitative: he prefers to listen to the group discuss each other's drafts and to chime in when he thinks the discussion is going astray or when he wants to add an important point. His small-group conferences are quite successful; students like their informal feel and say they get a lot of good feedback from their peers.

Chris always begins his courses with a personal narrative assignment. He believes that narrative helps students to think about their writing processes, and he likes the way he can rely on memories as occasions for introducing methods for discovering ideas, elaborating or exploring them, and then articulating them in vivid, stylish prose.

This time around, however, he wanted to try something new. He knew that model readings used for imitation have been out of fashion for some time in composition, and he knew that such modeling cannot be solidly supported theoretically. But something about using model readings kept tugging at him; he liked the way the students could *see* an author's use of personal memories and experiences as they thought about writing their own narratives. He decided to experiment a little, recasting his usual narrative assignment as follows:

First Assignment: Personal Narrative

For this first assignment, please select a reading by a professional author that you would like to model your own narrative on. You are free to choose whomever you like— select a reading you've seen before, or else "read around" a little until you find something appealing. Your "professional" narrative may even be a piece of fiction, as long as there is a narrator who is describing a specific experience that happened to him or her.

In your own narrative, be sure to follow our in-class techniques for elaborating specific events and memories. Use especially the technique of taking generalized events and then listing specific features beneath them to embellish your memories. Try to <u>feel</u> the event or action; try to <u>see</u> it; try to <u>hear</u> it; try to <u>re-create and reexperience</u> it. The life of a narrative is in <u>detail</u>—don't forget the cardinal rule of showing, not telling.

Please bring four <u>extra</u> copies of your rough draft on Friday.

On Friday morning, Chris devoted a few minutes at the end of his class session to what he calls the "paper shuffle," when each group trades drafts. In the midst of the paper shuffle, he handed out his peer-revision guide, a list of ten questions focusing on the characteristics of good narratives. The students were to fill these guides out for each of their peers' papers so that each writer would receive fully articulated commentary from three other readers.

On Tuesday morning, Chris got to the student union cafeteria twenty minutes before his first conference group was scheduled to meet. He liked waiting until shortly before the group meeting to read quickly through each batch of four papers, because without much time for reflection he would be less likely to dominate the discussion.

As he glanced at the names on the drafts, Chris remembered that this was his "loose ends" group, formed last because of the students' extremely tight schedules (8:00 a.m. being the only time when they all could meet). Chris knew that this group in particular would need some special attention, first because there was a gender imbalance (three men plus himself, and only one woman), and second because the students' personal profiles showed that the three men were all from rural settings and seemed rather young and naïve (none, for example, had visited a large city more than once or twice), while Anna Piel, the woman in the group, had lived all her life in the city and was worldly-wise and street-smart. Chris's quick reading of the papers written by the young men confirmed his expectations: John Campa's paper was a bland account of his grandmother's death, loosely modeled on a story by a writer Chris did not recognize. Keith Jackson's paper was an equally sophomoric description of a summer job he took in high school as a roofer, modeled on a fragment from Studs Terkel's book *Working*. And Richard Wilson's paper told of an expedition he and three friends made into a national park on a cold weekend when they had a hard time lighting a fire, Jack London's famous story being the authorial model.

Then Chris turned to Anna's draft, which began like this:

> I was living in a house with three guys and two girls in the summer of my third year after high school. We were all doing 'cid [LSD] and smoking dope until our brains were nowhere, and this is a story about how I was introduced to group sex and learned to go down on men and women at the same time. At first going down on women and guys together was scary but then it started to blow my mind.

After reading this paragraph, Chris felt mixed emotions. He was taken aback by Anna's forthrightness, but he was eager, in an almost voyeuristic way, to read on. At the same time, he was concerned that Anna had taken too many liberties with his assignment. He also wondered how the three shy young men would respond. Flipping to the end of Anna's long paper, he discovered a photocopied page, stapled to the draft, from one of Henry Miller's novels. It was a vivid account of the narrator's experience soliciting and then engaging in sex with a prostitute in Paris.

Returning to Anna's draft, Chris was shocked to find, as he read on, that she had described not one but six different sexual encounters with men and women, sometimes alone, sometimes in groups, in detail that would make the most explicit pornographic magazines sound like *Winnie-the-Pooh*. Anna had apparently used all the brainstorming and detail-enhancing techniques to elaborate her experiences with the most vivid minutiae of sound, smell, sight, taste, and touch. While Chris thought himself a fairly experienced reader who had, in his thirty-four years, seen more than a few genres of text, Anna's draft was so explicit that he found himself instinctively leaning over it a little and checking around to see if anyone else was nearby. By the time he had finished the draft, he felt completely conflicted—aroused by Anna's erotic descriptions, amazed by her meticulous detail, thoroughly engaged in her unusual story, guilty that he had succumbed in this way, worried about his teacherly role, and utterly confused about how to respond.

A few minutes after Chris had skimmed through to the end of Anna's paper, the group members began to arrive, first John and Rich, then Anna, who dropped her books confidently on the table, and finally Keith, flustered from catching a late bus. When everyone had gotten something from the cafeteria line and sat down to discuss the papers, Chris noticed that the three men were making little eye contact with him, with each other, or with Anna. They seemed to be waiting for Chris to say something, and it was clear that Anna's paper had created some tension in the group. Anna, for her part, seemed in high spirits and had displayed the papers and revision guides around her in anticipation of a lively and fruitful discussion.

Still dazed, Chris looked tentatively around the table. "Okay," he asked, "who wants to begin?"

ISSUES FOR DISCUSSION

• If you were Chris, how would you respond to Anna's paper in light of the assignment? Is Anna "wrong" to describe an unusual sexual experience? If Anna has, in fact, demonstrated all of Chris's criteria for successful narratives, including expertly elaborated descriptions, does Chris have a right to criticize her choice of "event" to practice these techniques?

• If you were to use Chris's assignment, would you want to forestall a paper like Anna's? Could you do that by modifying the assignment in terms of audience or purpose?

• Chris did not expect Anna's paper; as an audience (and creator of the assignment), he has certain expectations about what is appropriate to write about in his class. But teachers often refer to the entire class as the "audience" for students' writing. Imagine that Chris runs the group conference and the three young men confess that they loved Anna's story and were attracted to her vivid details. Whose "criteria" for appropriate writing should be privileged under these circumstances: the students' or Chris's? Why? How could your answer to this question be made clearer to students in Chris's assignment?

• In his assignment, should Chris have specified the ways that the readings ought to be taken as models, perhaps asking students to practice using his guide by identifying "characteristics of good narratives" in the models they chose? Anna apparently used the professional reading she chose as a model for her *subject*. Is it appropriate to use professional readings as subject models?

• Highly constraining assignments can avoid unwelcome responses but may also stifle creativity. Is it more important to invite students to take risks and be imaginative or to keep them reigned in? Why?

• On the basis of your discussions of the scenarios in this chapter, construct a list of do's and don'ts for creating effective writing assignments. Afterwards, compare lists with a colleague or a group of colleagues. What similarities do you notice? What differences?

Note

1. A version of assignments 1 and 2 appears in *Constellations: A Contextual Reader for Writers,* edited by John Schilb, Elizabeth Flynn, and John Clifford (New York: HarperCollins, 1992), 159, 477.

2 Using Readings
in Writing Courses

What is the role of readings in writing courses? Because the primary goal of a writing course is to engage students with their own writing, we may feel uneasy using writing by published authors. We may worry that we will have to spend so much time with the reading that we will neglect our students' texts. Some of our students may feel so intimidated by published readings that they will dismiss their own texts as unworthy by comparison.

The first scenario in this chapter presents an attempt to select and use a reading that is not intimidating and that helps students develop a sense of audience and reader response as well as an awareness of how readers depend on cues from writers. The second scenario asks about the appropriate relationship between reading material and students' own lives and experiences: Should students be faulted for not "relating" readings to their own experiences? Conversely, should students respond to readings predominantly in an "academic" or expository, analytical mode without recourse to their own histories? The third scenario then raises issues of ownership and creativity in a situation where students "rewrite" or "finish" existing works of literature. This scenario also asks about the appropriateness of using literary works as the readings for writing courses. Behind the final scenario are a number of general questions about the use of readings in composition. If we assign readings, how should they be ordered: by topic? by genre? according to whose choice? What kinds of writing assignments should readings lead to? What sorts of rhetorical issues emerge from writing about readings? In this scenario, three peer-teachers each design an assignment based on the same reading.

In answering the questions raised about readings, we need to draw upon our beliefs about cognition, student needs and development, cultural diversity, and the world in general.

Is There a Text in This Cartoon?

On the first day of his lower-division composition class, Jeffrey Philmore assured his students that the main focus of the course would be on their own writings and that they would be writing several drafts of each essay in the light of conferences and peer reviews. He also told the students they would be reading essays in a reader, and he urged them to believe that by reading these essays they would learn the variety of topics and strategies already-published writers use to engage readers in their writing situations. Jeffrey added that by reading already-written essays during the process of writing, writers become more aware of how readers respond to texts and why.

After making these preliminary remarks and going over his syllabus, Jeffrey gave the first assignment. He asked the students to read the school newspaper's editorial, cartoon, and letters to the editor in the back-to-school issue and be prepared to discuss the choice of topics and arguments in each text.

Jeffrey chose these texts rather than any in the reader because the back-to-school issue dealt with matters of immediate student interest. He also thought the texts were short enough to help him highlight several points he wanted to make: (1) readers find clues about a writer's assumptions and arguments in the context and genre of a text; (2) readers construct texts not just from the printed word, but also from personal memories, schemata, and inferences; (3) readers usually extend or modify a response to a text after reading or hearing other responses.

To help his students prepare for the assignment, Jeffrey distributed a cartoon from the previous term's back-to-school issue (Figure 1). He began by asking, "Does everyone agree that this cartoon's main argument is that campus parking is a problem?" The students all appeared to agree. When he asked how they made the inference, most singled out the number of cars in the background, the swearing driver, the screeching car, the ironic sign, and the back-to-school context. Some also offered their own stories to support the point that, because of lack of campus parking spaces, students have to waste time searching for a place to park and feel angry with drivers who cut in. Quite a few students admitted that they openly swear at the cut-ins.

Jeffrey also asked whether the cartoon would have conveyed the same argument if it did not picture the screeching car and the swearing driver. Most agreed that the argument would have been the same, but would have taken longer for a viewer to infer and would have been less memorable. Jeffrey then asked whether they thought a description of the scene or a written account by an individual trying to find a parking space would make the argument as effectively. Some students replied that only the cartoon could have such an immediate impact. Others claimed that individual stories would be just as effective because they are more personal than the cartoon and probably more specific.

Dismayed, on checking his watch, that class time was running out, Jeffrey quickly urged the students to note how they infer arguments in the readings for the next assignment, how valid they find the arguments, and how effective the arguments are as presented. To end the session, he asked the students in the remaining few minutes to write a brief "letter to the editor" about any campus problem in need of attention and solution.

Because the discussion had been lively and most of the students had participated in some way, Jeffrey was surprised to find when reading the "letters" that one student, Rosalie, protested. She wrote:

> *Looking at this cartoon was silly. I thought we were going to read about writing sentences and pargraphs. Any kid could understand this cartoon. And I don't see why the university has to be laughed at. It gives a parking lot for drivers to lazy to walk or bike. I walk or take the bus. And the carton is manely for males. The driver is a male, and most students defending him swearing are males. I hope we start reading stuff without swear words.*

ISSUES FOR DISCUSSION

• Do you agree with Rosalie that the cartoon is too obvious to be worth class attention? Why or why not?

CRAIG BAXTER

Figure 1. Cartoon from the back-to-school issue of the school newspaper. Reprinted by permission of Craig Baxter.

• What do you think Jeffrey was trying to accomplish in using a cartoon in this class? What if he had introduced, say, three cartoons— one very easy to get, one accessible for some students, and one likely to stump the whole class?

• Jeffrey believes that cartoons make a reader's constructive role especially evident. Will students be able to connect what they learn by reading cartoons to reading, say, each other's drafts? How could Jeffrey explain this connection further?

• Is it ever appropriate for a teacher to impose a meaning on a text used in a writing course? If so, when? Is Jeffrey's class such a situation?

• Should Jeffrey respond directly to Rosalie by writing a comment on her "letter"? by asking to speak with her? Should he deal with the content of her note only? with her attitude? with her usage and spelling problems? Or should he ignore the note?

• Should Jeffrey bring up the issue Rosalie raised when the class meets again? If so, should he use Rosalie's statements verbatim? Should he identify her as the source?

Balancing Lives and Texts

Adriana Sanchez and Chanley Young were teaching sections of expository writing at a large urban university. In their courses, they both chose to emphasize the relationships between reading and writing, using model essays to spark interest, to reveal various stylistic and structural patterns, and to provide material for papers in which the students would relate their own experiences, beliefs, or ideas to those presented by the authors.

In the scenarios that follow, Adriana's and Chanley's use of readings in the contexts of their students' lives raises important questions about the ways in which professional texts are used at various points—and in various ways—in students' creation of their own essays.

Moved by Language

Adriana's students, like those in most classes on her campus, were diverse in ethnicity, race, and age. She thought that students would become more sympathetic to this diversity if, for their first major essay, they compared their own school experience with the school experience of another person. Several selections in the course reader described such experiences from various cultural perspectives.

Early in the course, Adriana assigned three textbook readings that she hoped would evoke memories and experiences among the students that they could shape into personal essays on similar themes. The first, Theodore Sizer's "What High School Is," describes the experiences of Mark, an average student in a typical American high school. The second, Alice Walker's "Everyday Use," tells of Dee, a bright college graduate returning to her rural black community, and contrasts her experience with that of Maggie, her seemingly less bright but talented sister who had been schooled there. The third essay, Richard Rodriguez's "Aria: A Memoir of a Bilingual Childhood," recalls the author's boyhood conflict as he tried to assimilate English into his native Spanish.

On the day after assigning these selections, Adriana asked the students to break into groups and talk about the readings. The discussions were lively and productive and led nicely into Adriana's brief journal-writing episode at the end of the class.

For the next class, Adriana asked the students to bring first drafts of the essays for peer review and subsequent revision. To help the students prepare for the group work, she handed out the following questions for peer critique:

> Please respond to the following questions about the draft of each writer in your group:
>
> 1. Is the comparison between the writer's own experience and the experiences of Mark, Dee, Maggie, or Rodriguez clear to you?
>
> 2. Does the writer provide enough detail about the reading(s) he or she chose so that someone who has not read the selection(s) will have a general understanding of their content?
>
> 3. Does the writer provide enough detail about his or her own experience so that you can imagine and follow it? Is it vivid and moving enough?

At the end of the peer review hour, one student, Kevinder Singh, asked to talk to Adriana. Kevinder was an older student returning from the workplace to complete his degree in engineering. Visibly distressed, he argued that the other members of his peer group were following her guidelines too literally because they said his comparison with Rodriguez was not clear. Holding his paper carefully in front of him, as if it were a piece of fine china, he told Adriana that he thought he had *implied* the comparison instead of "beating it into their heads."

Kevinder's draft follows.

> Richard Rodriguez in his essay "Aria: A Memoir of a Bilingual Childhood" describes the experiences a bilingual child has to go through. I am also a bilingual child that experienced a childhood that was very unpleasent because I was isolated from public society.

At home, I experienced a childhood that was pleasent and safe. I knew my native language well and so did my entire family. My native language was my private language because it was a language me and my family only were familiar with, and it was a language that separated us from public society. When my parents spoke to me with the native tongue, I listened and became involved in the conversation because I understood what was being said; but when I opened the door to the outside world, things were totally different.

When I started elementary school, I was isolated and discriminated. Everyone was speaking a language that sounded like sounds that made no sense. I tried to put these sounds together, but they did not seem to make complete thoughts. I was isolated from the public because I spoke English poorly, and I feared the outside world greatly. Nobody talked to me, and I talked to no one. In class, I was the least noticed child because I was so quiet. I prayed everyday that the teacher would not call on me to answer a question I could not even understand. I looked forward to the end of school everyday so I could go home where I was no longer a stranger.

I later began understanding the English language and becoming part of society, but a good part of my childhood was spent fearing the public language. I received help from many teachers, and I thank them for accepting me and making me part of the public society. Now I can write this essay for an English class with great confidence because I believe in myself, and I believe I can do anything if I try. I can now complete thoughts without hesitation. It seems now that the English language has now become my native tongue.

ISSUES FOR DISCUSSION

• Responding to a story by telling another story is common in many cultures. Furthermore, Kevinder seems fully aware that he has compared his own experience with that of Rodriguez by implication only. Should he be required to make the comparison explicit, engaging the reading directly? Why or why not?

• Adriana sees that Kevinder feels strongly about the value of what he has written. Should she suggest ways he could improve the narrative of his own experience, ignoring the issue of comparison with the readings?

• One of Adriana's colleagues says that writing courses should use readings as occasions for critical thinking, but another colleague says that readings should serve only to suggest topics that students might want to write about. Are both uses of readings appropriate? appropriate in the same course? appropriate as alternatives on the same assignment?

• The guidelines Adriana distributed call for comparison, summary, and narration. Could the guidelines be improved so that students would readily see how these elements can be related to each other, that is, how they can integrate their own experience with an experience they have read about in a unified essay?

Where Do I Stand?

To encourage discussion, Chanley Young asked the students in her freshman composition class to divide into groups according to the topic unit in the reader that they were most interested in writing about for the second essay. The students chose to divide by the following topics: violence in schools, genetic engineering, and euthanasia.

Chanley asked the students to write essays on how any one or two of the readings in the reader had answered or raised some questions about their own positions on the topic. She also let each person in a group select the reading(s). To guide the students through the assignment, Chanley handed out the following "process" sheet:

Process Sheet: Personal Essay Based on Readings

1. Choose two readings in your topic area to respond to in your paper.

2. Read and summarize your two readings (summaries due next Monday), and draft a set of at least three questions to guide group discussion.

3. Discuss your group's readings in class (Monday) on the basis of your collective questions.

4. Following your discussion, begin shaping your summary into a reaction essay. In this essay, you will be responding to the experiences and arguments presented in the readings you have chosen. Feel welcome to draw on any personal experiences related to this issue.

5. A full draft of your reaction essay is due on Wednesday.

On Monday, Chanley was pleased with the group work: the students gave clear presentations of their summaries and stimulated discussion. But one group that had chosen euthanasia as its topic was struggling with only two members. The third student, Clay Jameson, had left a note in Chanley's box explaining that he would be absent to be by his grandfather's bedside when the doctors removed life-support equipment that had sustained him for almost two months as he battled pancreatic cancer.

When she returned to her office, Chanley found Clay's paper, which one of his friends had left in her mailbox. As she glanced through his draft, Chanley realized that, while giving clear summaries about the position of two essays he read on euthanasia, Clay was not clear about his own position or all that is involved in cases when a patient is unconscious. Yet she hesitated to be too critical, given Clay's personal circumstances. Furthermore, she was impressed with the details he had given and with his sympathetic treatment of the topic, but found it almost astonishing that Clay would have chosen to ignore all of his obviously extensive personal experience with the right-to-die issue and stick only to the readings.

Clay's first draft follows.

In 1988, an intern wrote an essay defending his use of morphine to end the life of Debbie, a 20 year old terminally ill patient, dying in great pain from cancer and pleading, "Let's get this over with." But this intern viewed Debbie's case only once. How much knowledge could he have possibly gathered? His decision should have been made by Debbie's usual doctor and agreed upon by her relatives. I believe that such a drastic step as euthanasia should be taken only when all other treatment fails.

But like the intern, I don't believe that euthanasia should be exterminated completely. Why should a terminally ill patient dying of cancer live out a long life of pain when death is imminent and inescapable and he or she could be laid to rest in peace? If a person writes a living will (a will which states that if a person is surviving only because of a life support machine, than that person should be taken off this machine and allowed to die), than the wishes of this person should be granted. For example, if in the future, I ever write out a living will and for some reason I have to be hooked up to a life support machine, I hope the doctor in my case will take me off the machine. I believe that a person does have the right to choose his or her future.

For example, there is Sidney Hook. Hook defends euthanasia in his essay, "In Defense of Voluntary Euthanasia." In his essay, Hook writes about a violent heart attack that he experienced a few years ago. In his essay, he points out how much pain and suffering occurred during his recovery. He says, "Violent and painful hiccups, uninterupted for several days and nights, prevented the ingestion of food. My left side and one of my vocal cords became paralyzed. Some form of pleurisy set in, and I felt I was drowning in a sea of slime." During these days of agony, he asked his physician to discontinue all life-support services. His Doctor refused, and within six months he was almost fully recovered.

Now that I look at the case and see that Hook is fully recovered, I have to agree with the decision that the doctor made to not apply euthanasia to Hook. The only reason that I side with the doctor is because life is worth more than anything else in the world. But if I got to view the case before

Hook's recovery, I would have to side with Hook. I think Hook should have been taken off life support like he requested. He should have been able to choose his own future.

   To conclude, Euthanasia can benefit us all if it is used under the right circumstances. Through writing, many authors like the intern and Hook can express their views. Even though I don't totally agree with all their views I think that each author had good support to back up their views. Without euthanasia, patients like Debbie would have to live long lives of pain.

ISSUES FOR DISCUSSION

• When students read extensively about a topic, their thinking about it usually becomes—should become—more complex. Creating a coherent argument of their own therefore becomes more difficult. When teachers evaluate essays based on readings, should they place a higher value on the coherence of students' arguments or on students' efforts to deal with complexities? Should the priority be the same in responding to drafts and to final copies?

• If Chanley could ask Clay just three questions about what the readings say or the ways he has used the readings, what should her questions be?

• Should instruction value cogent analysis and synthesis of assigned readings over less "academic" and possibly more emotional and personal reactions? Why or why not?

Re-creating the Creation

Toward the middle of the term of a freshman composition class, Bill Chung, a first-year teaching assistant, was beginning to get a bit depressed. He was concerned by what he saw as colorless and lifeless writing in his students' papers, so he decided to try a teaching technique that one of his faculty mentors recommended to him: he would ask his students to rewrite a poem or part of a short story, incorporating in their re-creation some ideas from essays they had discussed in class. They were to turn in both their re-creation and a brief justification, explaining what ideas they were trying to incorporate in it. Bill, who considered himself a pretty staunch liberal pacifist, asked the students to work with one of several poems and short stories that deal with issues of peace and civil disobedience.

   Bill was particularly impressed by the effort one student, Yvonne Hughes, put into this assignment. Yvonne rewrote Claude McKay's poem "If We Must Die," drawing upon Sojourner Truth's defense of women in her essay, "Ain't I a Woman?" Despite his enthusiasm for Yvonne's effort, however, Bill was somewhat uneasy over her use of warlike metaphors to express her desire as a member of the women's soccer team to defeat its main rivals, the Tigers. Moreover, in class he had made a point to connect McKay's poem to the first stirrings of a civil rights movement among Harlem writers in the 1920s, but Yvonne in her accompanying justification explicitly linked McKay's poem to World War I. Bill was not sure how to comment on these features or grade them, nor was he sure whether he should comment on the few usage errors (a comma splice, a fragment) since Yvonne had so clearly enjoyed working on the re-created poem and explanation.

Here is the original poem by Claude McKay:

If We Must Die[1]

If we must die, let it not be like hogs
Hunted and penned in an inglorious spot,
While round us bark the mad and hungry dogs,
Making their mock at our accursed lot.
If we must die, O let us nobly die,
So that our precious blood may not be shed
In vain; then even the monsters we defy
Shall be constrained to honor us though dead!
O kinsmen! We must meet the common foe!
Though far outnumbered let us show us brave,
And for their thousand blows deal one deathblow!
What though before us lies the open grave?
Like men we'll face the murderous, cowardly pack,
Pressed to the wall, dying, but fighting back.
                                        (1919)

Here are Yvonne's poem and the accompanying justification:

Yvonne Hughes
"If We Must Lose"

If we must lose, let it not be like babies
Hunted and squeezed in a playpen,
Surrounded by tigers foaming with rabies,
Making us fools over and over again.
If we must lose, O let us nobly lose,
So that our score is always quite tight;
Then even though winners they would choose
Not to play us again for they know how we fight!
O teammates! We want to beat the common foe!
Though they are cooler let us not choke,
And for their thousand slams deal one deathblow!
Or what lies before us but one endless joke?
Like warriors we'll face the intimidating pack,
Pressed to the net, killing balls, fighting back!!

My poem "If we must lose" imitates fairly closely the form
and idea of Claude McKay's poem, "If we must die". I had to
choose this topic becuase the Tiger's team made me angry in
the last two weeks becuase it defeated the soccer team I play
on twice. Since our defeat, I had to think about this team and
our next chance to play them again the following weekend.
We have to make sure that we are, indeed, the better team,
the stronger group which holds together when there is one
last chance to win.

The other essay I wanted to work with is Sojourner Truth's
essay "Ain't I a Woman", her story is fascinating and moving
because she is a very strong person who neither accepted
physical inferiority of women nor the idea that they should be
placed on pedestals; nor did she subordinate women's rights
to the pursuit of racial equality.

My next step is to show how these three things (McKay's
poem, my poem, and Sojourner Truth's essay) are connected.
McKay's poem is mostly concerned with men, fighting against
each other. Understandable because he wrote it in 1922, so a
few years after the first World War. "Like men we'll face the
murderous, cowardly pack/ Pressed to the wall, dying, but
fighting back!" McKay in these lines pictures men in leading
positions, in which, they never give up and still fight back,
even though there is no way out.

My poem turns these ideas being in the leading position
and never giving up around and applying them to women in a
nontraditional role. I shall prove that women are not only good
at wearing high-heels and staying in the kitchen looking after
the babies, and I shall also prove that especially in sports,
women can demonstrate the qualities which are normally associated with men, like strength, competitiveness, bravery and
physical power. Our team will give everything to our rivals to
show our power too often just associated with men-teams.

Truth's story inspires women to be strong and fight for
their rights. That leads to the same opinion I have, that
women should never hide behind men but find their own way.
As Truth says, "Nobody ever helps me into carriages, . . . , or
gives me any best place! I could work as much and eat as
much as a man—when I could get it—and bear the lash as
well! And ain't I a woman?" Or in another paragraph, she
mentions: "If the first woman God ever made was strong
enough to turn the world upside down all alone, these women
together ought to be able to turn it back, and get right side up
again! And now they are asking to do it, the men better let
them."

ISSUES FOR DISCUSSION

• What do you think Bill was trying to accomplish with this assignment?

• Is the literary nature of this assignment appropriate for a writing
course? Why or why not?

• Yvonne's poem and justification incorporate aspects that seem counter to Bill's emphasis in class. If Bill were to raise his concerns about this, either in a group of instructors or to you personally, how would you respond to him?

• In the days of Shakespeare, re-creating a text was not questioned. In this day of copyright laws and affirmation of ownership, should an instructor encourage students to rewrite a poem or change an ending to a story? How can this kind of assignment be defended?

• No instructors in courses in other disciplines ask students to recreate texts already written. Should an instructor in a writing course assign such a task?

• Does such an assignment place students in the class in opposition, with those who are able to re-create a text creatively being evaluated more favorably than those who can analyze and explicate a text effectively?

• Yvonne clearly got very involved in this assignment. Should Bill comment in any way on matters of grammar and diction in her writing, considering that she was in the throes of creativity?

Three Ways of Looking at a Reading Assignment

Jack Ricka, Carol Moore, and Tony Smith were three teaching assistants in the same writing program. Jack and Tony, graduate students from the history department, were assigned teaching assistantships in the writing program. Carol was an English graduate student. As part of a collaborative project in their "Teaching Writing" seminar, these three instructors had teamed up to select two readings. Each instructor would then design an assignment or assignment sequence around the two readings, write a rationale for their choices, and compare the different ways in which they used the readings in their assignments. The essays they chose were Ken Ringle's "Ellis Island: The Half Opened Door" and Jane Tompkins's "At the Buffalo Bill Museum—June 1988." A summary of the two essays follows.

September 7, 1990, marked the opening of the new Ellis Island Museum commemorating the history of immigration to America. Ken Ringle, a *Washington Post* reporter, took the occasion to write an essay, "Ellis Island: The Half Opened Door," about Americans' history of ambivalence toward immigrants. He portrays America's love-hate relationship in an article that describes the "nativist sentiments which flared with each surge of immigration" and contrasts those feelings to our historical pride in welcoming those who provided the "human energy that would fuel the farms and factories of a growing nation." Ringle's article is packed with telling details describing how newcomers were "processed" through Ellis Island. In one painfully specific paragraph, he tells of the "eye men" who used buttonhooks to pull back eyelids of new arrivals to check for infection. In this way, he both personalizes and objectifies the experience, choosing his details carefully, yet letting them speak for themselves, with little overt commentary on his part.

Ringle moves his argument from the museum to the current debate over Hispanic immigration and asks: "Do we embrace the politics of hope or the politics of fear? [The Ellis Island Museum raises] the most basic and troubling of human questions, for what is our immigration debate other than that most primal human struggle between the instincts of socialization and those of territoriality?"

Jane Tompkins also uses a museum as the springboard for asking troubling questions about Americans' self-concept in her essay, "At the Buffalo Bill Museum—June 1988." She recounts a visit she made to the Buffalo Bill Historical Center in June of 1988. During her tour of the museum, she shares with the reader her stumbling discoveries about history and her own reactions to those discoveries. She moves from first person narrative in the beginning of the essay to direct address (you) in the latter part.

At the opening Tompkins writes that, in spite of the "fresh-faced young attendants wearing badges, . . . and the well designed and well run [museum itself]—a haven of satiny marble, shining mirrors and flattering light," the Buffalo Bill Museum was "one of the most disturbing places I have ever visited" (526). Her essay moves as a personal journey through the rooms full of Frederic Remington's works, and she comments on the "brutality of their subject matter." The paintings and statues in the exhibit "embody everything that was objectionable about this era in American history. They are imperialist and racist; they glorify war and the torture and killing of animals; there are no women in them anywhere" (528).

In the second part of the essay, Tompkins visits the Plains Indian Museum, "a terrible letdown" compared with the building housing the Remingtons. The artifacts and the presentation were so low-key as to be almost incomprehensible to her. There was no introductory video, no polished corridors, only scraps of buffalo hide and lifeless manikins standing in front of featureless teepees. "The deeper purpose of the museum began to puzzle me," she writes. "What is an Indian museum for, anyway? Why should we be bothering to preserve the vestiges of a people whose culture we had effectively extinguished? Wasn't there an air of bad faith about this? Did the museum exist to assuage our guilt and not for any educational reason?" (536).

In the third part of the essay, Tompkins describes her visit to the Winchester Arms Museum and is horrified by the glorification of the weapons and the purposes for which they were used.

Throughout the first three parts of this long essay, Tompkins expresses a growing sense of "moral outrage" and "indignation." Yet she adds a surprising coda to her essay. After her visit to the Buffalo Bill Historical Center, she begins to read about the real Bill Cody and discovers a man of uncommon "courage, daring, strength, endurance, generosity, openness to other people, love of drama, [and] love of life" (544). She writes, "I found myself unable to sustain the outrage that I had felt on leaving the museum—it made me reflect on the violence of my own reaction" to the historical center (544–5). She ends the essay unable, finally, to resolve the contradiction between her experience of the museums and her own research—aware that if "[you don't] come to recognize the violence in yourself and your own anger and your own destructiveness, whatever else you do won't work" (545).

The three teachers approached these two essays quite differently. As you read through their rationales, think about how you might have responded to this task. Try to evaluate whether these approaches are equally useful for a writing class. Consider the question: If we each bring a unique context to our reading, how does one teacher's "take" on a particular essay influence how he or she uses it in class?

Jack Ricka's Rationale

After reading the two essays, I find it hard to imagine a way to teach these essays in conjunction with one another. Perhaps they both show the ambiguities of what it means to be an American, or some such vague moral lesson, but both in subject and style, the two essays have little in common.

If I must teach them together, I would envision a unit on "What it means to be an American," and seek to develop two different writing assignments based on these essays. The first would address the question: What does it mean to be a member of a community? I would have them write a paper describing themselves as a member of a particular community, perhaps incorporating a discussion of definition—what is an American? I might point out that both essays in some way discuss alienation from the mainstream, although from different angles.

A second possible writing assignment would direct students to write a description of one of the two museums from the point of view of either the Plains Indians or the immigrants. This exercise would give students the experience of reinterpreting information by placing it in a different frame. We would discuss how the shift affects the students' sense of audience, purpose, and relevant details in their own writing.

I'd rather teach them separately, though, because I think Jane Tompkins's essay is so wordy and disorganized that it would provide a great exercise in editing! The piece has no clear thesis, and no logical flow. I might break up my class into groups devoted to revising the essay for a particular audience—history students, for example. I'd teach the Ringle article as an example of a researched argument. His use of sources and details propel his argument forward.

Tony Smith's Rationale

I see both of these essays as a particularly useful means of presenting students with history in ways which may incite them to write. Both confront popular myths about our country's past. The "Wild West" and the "Open Door" have become cliches, and these readings take familiar ideas and challenge them in fundamental ways. I'd like to use these readings as a springboard for discussion about the relationship between myth and history, and the relationship of the present with the past.

For writing, I'd have my students choose a museum to visit, and have them write about the things they would expect to see based on their knowledge of the subject. Then I'd have them go to the museum of their choice, take notes, and write a paper comparing their "before and after" impressions.

Carol Moore's Rationale

First of all, I think these two essays are examples of sophisticated writing, and I wouldn't want to introduce them until the second part of the course. I'd like to draw attention to the ways the two writers present volatile issues without provoking knee-jerk objections from their audiences. They are both skilled at establishing relationships with their readers and moving toward controversy only gradually.

Ringle, for example, nurses his relationship with his readers when he calls early attitudes toward immigrants "ambivalence." His choice of words is important (he didn't use "animosity" for example). He uses rhetorical strategies to convince his readers to trust him and his interpretation of the facts, calling on John F. Kennedy, and other sources to establish his "ethos."

Jane Tompkins also deals with a touchy chapter in American history. She establishes her relationship with her readers by leading us through the museum as if we are by her side.

Her use of "I" and "you" and the rhetorical questions sprinkled throughout the essay draw us into her argument and make it hard to disagree with her conclusions.

After discussing these rhetorical strategies with my classes, I would ask them to try this type of argumentation. They might try to write an argument to a hostile audience (presenting a pro-choice position to a pro-life audience, for example). How would they establish a relationship with their readers? How would they present the facts of their case? Can they present their conclusions in a way that would be accepted by their readers?

ISSUES FOR DISCUSSION

• One question that arises when teaching readings in a writing class is whether the teacher should focus on the subject or content of the readings or on the rhetorical strategies of the authors. Jack and Tony tended to focus on the content, while Carol dealt almost entirely with the rhetoric of the two pieces. In your opinion, who has the more effective approach here?

• Looking at Jack's discussion, should a writing teacher ask students to "edit" the work of a recognized (published) author? Why or why not?

• Tony has an interesting idea about sending students to do a kind of "ethnographic" research in actual museums. In addition to having his students read the two essays, what instruction should Tony give them before he sends them into the field? Do you think writing classes should engage in "fieldwork," or should the focus stay primarily on texts?

• Carol designs a writing assignment that parallels the rhetorical nature of the essays, rather than drawing on their content. To what extent does this approach open unlimited topics for students to write about? To what extent does it limit topic-specific invention strategies? How closely should writing assignments based on readings stick to the topic of the reading?

Note

1. "If We Must Die" is reprinted by permission of the Archives of Claude McKay, Carl Cowl, admin. *Selected Poems of Claude McKay,* published by Harcourt Brace Jovanovich, 1969.

3 Responding to Student Writing

Perhaps nothing we do as teachers in the composition class affects the development of students' writing abilities as much as thorough, useful responses to their writing. In the traditional classroom, students received feedback mostly in the form of a final evaluation—often cursory, often critical, and, because it came too late to be put to use, usually not very instrumental in helping them improve their writing. Today, teachers find that students learn more about writing when they can receive thorough, readerly responses to drafts in progress and use these responses to make principled, effective revisions.

While it is clearly one of the most useful pedagogical tools we have, responding to students' writing also remains one of the most difficult and complex tools to use. Response takes many forms: oral feedback provided by an instructor during a private conference; written comments in the margins or at the end of a paper; reactions provided by peers in small-group revision conferences; suggestions on revision guides; tape-recorded commentary. Every time a teacher or fellow student reads and reacts to a student's paper, the social and interpersonal dimensions of the classroom come fully into play. Personalities can mesh productively—or clash. Advice can become the basis for effective revision—or it can be misinterpreted. Students can interpret and make excellent use of a teacher's reactions as they improve their writing, or those reactions can set up false expectations and frustration. Some kinds of response can completely rebuild a student's conception of how writing works; others can reinforce the most unproductive myths and attitudes. Good response can almost by itself help students to improve significantly as writers. Poor, unconsidered response can be not only ineffective, it can alienate, reduce self-esteem, or turn a student away from writing completely.

The scenarios in this chapter focus on various interpersonal, practical, and pedagogical dimensions of response as it occurs in six different contexts. The first scenario provides four versions of a student's draft with peer and teacher commentary and asks the reader to critique each set of comments. The second scenario provides transcriptions of oral comments during two teachers' small-group revision conferences and asks for a comparison of the teachers' agendas and methods. In the third scenario, a student's racist journal entry outrages his teacher and raises the issue of what response she should make to it. The fourth scenario describes a situation in which a male student uses his paper to challenge his young female instructor's authority and imply that he wants to have an affair with her. In the fifth scenario, a teacher confesses to one of her students that she will have trouble being fair in her evaluation of his work because his position on abortion is so opposed to hers; now she faces a possible lawsuit for violating his right to free speech. And in the final scenario a student goes beyond the boundaries of an assignment by writing a personal rather than an expository essay about a reading.

In each case, the nature, tone, medium, and content of response to students' writing become the central issues for discussion—punctuated by the no less important matters of gender, authority, student-teacher relationship, and instructional ideology.

Four Takes on a Student Essay

One

For their next-to-last writing assignment, George Kazakis asked his students to write an essay about a controversial issue. In doing so, the students were to use some personal experience to draw attention to a debate over the issue they selected. He guided his students through the writing process by first asking them to produce a preliminary set of notes or examples, using invention strategies they had already learned. They were then to bring this set of invention notes to class for preliminary review.

In the class session on the invention notes, George had each student work with a partner so that they could verbalize from their notes the connection between their personal experiences and at least two opposing arguments about their respective issues. At the end of this session, George told the students to revise their invention notes, using their partners' comments. During the next class, they would then write as much of a preliminary draft as they could from their notes.

By the end of that class session, Ava Johnson had produced the following preliminary draft of her essay. (This typed version is an exact reproduction of Eva's handwritten draft.)

> ~~The ba~~ The Franklin auditorium was filled to full capacity the night of Graduation. Everything had been arranged weeks in advance. As the valairctorian said the closing words to her

fare-well speech, two ~~best~~ good friends within the Graduating class embrace hands. These guys had been friends since the freshman year and was nothing alike. One ~~w~~ of them was the ~~Val~~ a middle-class white male. ~~Graduated at the top of his class in college~~ Graduated from college and High school with a 3.8 grade point average. He also had all the qualities to be successful ~~in~~ executive, ~~inlleg~~ intelligent, aggressive, assertive. The other guy was an okay student in high middle class Black school. Through minority programs, He was admitted into college. ~~He~~ After ~~is~~ alot of hard work ~~in the light~~ and ~~industry~~ standing, he graduated from college with a 3.0 grade point average. Both of these graduates will be pushed out into the real world to get a job and support themselves on the Knowledge ~~they~~ have acquired in college. But if both of these men apply for the same job, One could obviously ~~ele~~ choose this indivdual ~~for~~ that would be hired. It is obvious that the white man would be hired even though he is not the person who is fully qualified. How could it be possible for a black or an other minority to get good jobs that were once denied to them years ago. ~~T~~ The organization called affirmative action is the reason why. Affirmative action is an organization that requires businesses to hire a certain percentage of ~~blacks to business~~ minorities or colleges to admit so many blacks. Even though ~~these are~~ individuals state that racial discrimination is non-existence today, is affirmative action really needed in the occupational work place today. No matters how much progress ~~is~~ was made since the first day blacks and other minorities were given there first liberties, affirmative action is still needed in the work place.

~~The~~ AA is needed in the work place to intergrate the job market with women and minorities. The job market is currently monopolized with middle to upper class white males. ~~They~~ Through the ~~past~~ years, ~~bl~~ minorities and women were kept out because they couldn't fill the qualifications imposed by white men. By the demands proposed by AA, companies ~~were~~ had to hire more women and blacks.

Although AA is needed to speed up the flow of which women and minorities ~~are~~ put into the work force, it also breaks vicious cycle of minorities being ~~unqualified for certain positions~~ underqualified for certain positions. When a black is hired for a job position he or she may be unqualified because they didn't have ~~the a fallfilling~~ advantages during their upbringings. They were probably brought up in a home where there were an abundance of children. This face ~~would be~~ alone would put a limitation on the parental attention that one child would recieve. ~~The mother~~ Both parents probably worked and ~~the child didn't have~~ enough money to buy their children ~~the proper~~ adequate learning materials such as a personal computer or expensive educational games such as speak and spell. ~~They~~ This cycle continues through ~~of~~ each generation. But with AA, this ~~organization~~ action comes to a halt. ~~It~~ AA gets minorities out of these situations by putting them in better jobs so they can earn a higher income. When they earn a higher income, ~~thery children may~~ they might be able to provide their children with some advantages that they didn't have. ~~There are disadvantages to this~~ Although the job industry is getting flooded with inexperienced minorities, their children and ~~their~~ grandchildren ~~will be closer~~ an equalibrium ~~with the other races~~ will become more experienced, which will bring ~~the~~ all the races to an equilibruim when it comes to the job industry.

AA is not fair to everyone. It is almost a reverse form of the discrimination that people fought to destroy years ago. ~~But with everything, you can't make everyone happy.~~ (Explain how)

Two

After the students wrote their preliminary draft, George asked them to write a second draft by using at least two "revision tips" he handed out on a dittoed sheet:

Revision tips for Draft #2: (use at least two)

1. Emphasize the differences between various positions on your controversial issues. Make sure you think about different views.

2. Delete or add feelings so that the reader shares your own feelings or is persuaded to agree with your position on the issue.

3. Reorder paragraphs or examples for more effective persuasion.

4. Write a persuasive conclusion.

Please bring this second draft to class for review by a classmate.

A typed transcript of Ava's handwritten second draft appears below and is followed by the comments of Alicia Tolmach, Ava's peer-review partner.

The [university] Auditorium was filled to full capacity for the graduation of the [university] business majors. As the valedictorian said the closing words to her farewell speech, two good friends within the class embraced hands. ~~The guys had attended the college their freshman years. The guys~~ Both had been treated equally ~~although~~ college, but one will have a definite advantage over the other when it comes to appling for a job. One of the men ~~had graduated from high school and is~~ was ~~currently~~ graduating from college with a 3.8 grade point average. ~~He also possess the such qualities as aggressive He adapts well~~ He is adaptive, aggressive, ~~and~~ assertive, and he is also white. The other ~~guy~~ man, a middle class black, was ~~an okay student in high school and was~~ accepted into college through minority programs. after ~~alot~~ much hard work and long days, he graduated from college with a 3.0 grade point average.

~~Both of these graduates will be pushed out into the real world and in will have to support themselves on the Knowledge they have acquired in college.~~ ~~but~~ If both of these men apply for the same job, ~~and could obviously be hired over the others it would be~~ obviously ~~that~~ the white man would be hired because of his higher GPA ~~he is more qualified~~. But in some instances, the black man would be hired even though he is not of ~~the~~ highley ~~person who is fully~~ qualified. How could it be possible for minorities to get good jobs ~~that were once~~ denied to them years ago? the organization called affirmative action is the reason why ~~a~~ affirmative action ~~is an organization that~~ forces businesses to hire a certain percentage of minorities. even though racial discrimination is ~~non existence~~ less prevalent today than it has been in the past, Affirmative Action is still needed in the work place.

AA is needed ~~in the work place~~ to intergrate the job market with minorities. The job market is currently monopolized with middle to upper class white males. Through the years, minorities were kept out of the work industry because they couldn't fill the qualifications imposed by white men. By the coersion of AA, companies had to hire more ~~women and blacks~~ and hispanics.

~~Although~~ AA is needed to speed up the flow of ~~which~~ minorities being accepted into the work place, however, ~~it also~~ breaks ~~th~~ a vicious cycle of minorities being underqualified ~~for~~ when applying for certain job positions. When a black is hired for a job position, he may be unqualified because ~~they~~ didn't have as many advantages during ~~their~~ his life. ~~They were~~ He was probably brought up in a home with an abundance of children. that fact alone would put a limitation on the parental attention that one child would recieve. ~~Both the Household is up most likely a tw~~ Both parents probably worked and didn't have enough money to buy their children adequate learning materials such as a personal computer. this cycle is continued through each generation.

   In accord with the assignment, Alicia filled in the peer-review sheet that George distributed. Her comments on Ava's second draft follow.

MR. KAZAKIS
ENGLISH COMPOSITION
PEER-REVIEW SHEET: CONTROVERSIAL ISSUE ESSAY
REVIEWER'S NAME: *Alicia Tolmach*

1. Evaluate the way in which the writer introduces the controversy underlying the essay. Are two (or more) conflicting positions regarding the topic clearly defined? Explain your answer.

There are two conflicting positions within the essay. One position is when Affirmative Action is needed to integrate the work place. The other is the need to bring the majority of minorities above the poverty level.

2. How effectively does the writer use logic to advance his or her argument? Give an example of an explicitly stated application of logical reasoning in the essay. Evaluate the effectiveness of the example you choose. If you cannot find such an example, briefly discuss the extent to which you think the essay suffers as a result.

A perfect example of logical reasoning is when the writer stated the probability of minorities staying in poverty due to the lack of good jobs. The fact is very effective because it can be believed very easily. One can assume that money can have a great impact on someone's life, and without a good job, the possibilities of advancement are non-existent.

3. How well does the writer counter anticipated objections to his or her own arguments? Explain your answer.

The writer does not counter any objections to her arguments because the points the writer stated were very true.

4. Does the writer employ emotional language to support his or her argument? If not, is this a fault? If so, how effectively does the writer use emotional language to advance his or her argument? Explain your answer.

No. The writer does not need to bring emotions into play when she starts her essay. The content of the essay is enough to persuade the reader.

Three

At the end of the peer-review session, George had students sign up for a conference with him. For this conference, they were to bring a draft of their essay, revised in light of the peer review and their own independent thinking about persuasive writing. What follows is the draft Ava produced.

The [university] Auditorium was filled to full capacity for the graduation of the [university] business majors. As the valedictorian said the closing words to her farewell speech, two good friends within the class embraced hands. Both have been treated equally throughout college, but one will have a definite advantage over the other when it comes to applying for a job. One of the men is graduating from college with a 3.8 grade point average. He is adaptive, aggressive, assertive,

and he is also a caucasian. The other man, an Afro- American, was accepted into college through minority programs.
After strenuous hours and long days, he is embarking from
college with a 3.0 grade point average. With the skills and
knowledge both of these men have acquired from college, it
would be obvious that if both of those men apply for the
same job that, causasian would get it. but in some instances
today, the black man would be hired even though he is not as
highly qualified. How could it be possible for minorities,
whether qualified or unqualified, to get good jobs that were
denied to them years ago? The organization called Affirmative
Action is the reason why. Affirmative Action forces businesses
to hire a certain percentage of minorities to help eliminate
racial discrimination. even though racial discrimination is less
prevalent today than it has been in the past, Affirmative Action
is still needed in the work place.

Affirmative Action is needed to intergrate the job market
with minorities. The job market is currently monopolized with
middle to upper class white males. Through the years, minorities were kept out of work industry because they couldn't fill
the qualifications imposed by society. But with the coersion of
Affirmative Action, companies had to hire more minorities.

Although Affirmative Action speeds up the flow of Minorities
being accepted into the work place, it also breaks the vicious
cycle of minorities bring underqualified when applying for certain job positions. When a black is hired for a job position, he
may be unqualified because he did not have as many advantages during his life. He was probably brought up in a home
with an abundance of children. the fact alone would put a
limitation on the parental attention that one child would receive. Both parents probably worked and did not have enough
money to buy their children adequate learning materials, such
as a personal computer. This cycle of the minority parent and
minority child is continued throughout each generation. But
with Affirmative Action, this action comes to a halt. Affirmative
Action gets minorities out of these situations by putting them
in better jobs so they can earn a higher income. When they
earn a higher income, they might be able to provide their
children with some advantages that they did not have. Although the job industry is getting flooded with inexperienced
minorities, their children and grandchildren will become more
experienced with better living standards which will bring all
the races to an equilibrium in the years to come.

Affirmative Action is not fair to everyone. It is almost a
reverse form of the discrimination that people fought to destroy years ago. But, in time, the abilities of minorities will
improve and Affirmative Action will become non-existent.

Four

In conferences, George tries to inspire the students to make their own
revisions. He begins by asking the students to tell him about problems

they are still having with the essay. He then suggests that they brainstorm solutions together. If necessary, he gives his advice about how to solve problems. After listening, answering questions, and offering praise for work done so far, George has each student read at least the opening two paragraphs aloud for tone and style. After this reading, he has the student suggest what changes in diction or punctuation would be effective.

After her conference with George, Ava produced the following final draft.

Finally Promoted

The [university] Auditorium was filled to capacity for the graduation of the [ ] University business majors. As the valedictorian said the closing words of her farewell speech, two good friends within the class embraced hands. Both have been treated equally throughout college, but one will have a definite advantage over the other when it comes to applying for a job. One of the men is graduating from college with a 3.8 grade point average. He is adaptive, aggressive, assertive, and he is also a Caucasian. The other man, an Afro- American, was accepted into college through minority programs. After strenuous hours and long days, he is embarking from college with a 3.0 grade point average. With the skills and knowledge both these men have acquired from college, it would be obvious that if both apply for the same job, the Causasian would get it. In some instances today, however, the black man would be hired even though he is not as highly qualified.

How could it be possible for minorities, whether qualified or unqualified, to get good jobs that were denied to them years ago? The program called Affirmative Action is the reason. Affirmative Action forces businesses to hire a certain percentage of minorities to help eliminate discrimination. Even though discrimination is less prevalent today than it has been in the past, Affirmative Action is still needed in the work place.

Affirmative Action is needed to integrate the job market with minorities. The job market is currently monopolized with middle-to-upper-class white males. Through the years, minorities were kept out of the work place because they could not fulfill the qualifications imposed by society. But with the coersion of Affirmative Action, companies had to hire more minorities.

Although Affirmative Action speeds up the flow of Minorities being accepted into the work place, it also breaks the vicious cycle of minorities being underqualified when applying for certain job positions. When a black is hired for a job position, he may be unqualified because he did not have as many advantages during his life. He was probably brought up in a home with an abundance of children. That fact alone would put a limitation on the parental attention that one child would receive. Both parents probably worked and did not have enough money to buy their children adequate learning materials, such as a personal computer. This cycle of the minority parent and minority child is continued throughout each generation. But with Affirmative Action, this comes to a halt. Affirmative Action gets minorities out of these situations by putting them in better jobs so they can earn a higher income. When they earn a higher income, they might be able to provide their children with advantages they themselves did not have. Although the job industry is getting flooded with inexperienced minorities, their children and grandchildren will become more experienced and have better living standards which will bring all minorities to equilibrium in the years to come.

Affirmative Action is not fair to everyone. It is almost a reverse form of the discrimination that people fought to destroy years ago. But, in time, the abilities of minorities will improve and Affirmative Action will become unnecessary and nonexistent.

Bibliography

Neas, Ralph G. "Affirmative Action is working well" <u>USA Today</u> (Newspaper). 10 Nov. 1986: 9.

Rodriquez, Richard "None of this is Fair" <u>Lexington Reader</u>. D.C. Health and Company 1987. p. 361-365

Vaksdal, Diane L. "Nation Never Needed Affirmative Action" <u>USA Today</u> (Newspaper). 10 Nov. 1986: 9.

ISSUES FOR DISCUSSION

• Given the evolution of Ava's drafts, how would you evaluate the whole process George led his students through? In addition to collaborative brainstorming, written peer-review sheets, and teacher-student conferences, what other forms of response might be effective?

• If you were George, how would you have responded to the draft Ava brought to the conference? To what extent would you use Alicia's peer-review comments when you met with Ava?

• How effective are the questions on the peer-review sheet? How effective are the comments from the student peer reviewer?

• What are the advantages and disadvantages of having the conference after the peer review? Before the peer review?

• What should teachers do in class to prepare students to be good peer reviewers?

• Should a teacher award credit to peer reviewers for their work? Why or why not? If so, what criteria should a teacher use to evaluate peer review?

- Give a grade to Ava's final draft. To what extent does seeing the evolution of the drafts affect your judgment?

Two Teachers' Responses in Group Conferences

Eileen Xuan and Michael Hill are both teaching an introductory composition course. Both routinely use peer-group conferences as a way to help students read and respond to each other's papers, practice both major and minor revision, and develop sensitivity to audience. In their version of peer-group conferencing, Michael and Eileen prefer to facilitate small groups of three or four students by meeting with them in a casual setting, usually the student union. During the week of conferences, students must bring in rough drafts of their papers on Monday, exchange them, hand in one copy to the teacher, and then read and respond to each paper by using a revision guide designed to help them focus their attention on critical issues in their partners' drafts. Michael and Eileen cancel their regular classes on Wednesday and Friday and meet, one after another, with each of their seven groups. Each group meets for one hour, devoting roughly fifteen minutes to each student's paper.

Although they share many of the same beliefs about writing instruction, Michael and Eileen do not entirely agree on their roles in the conference groups. Eileen prefers to take a back seat during the meetings, listening to the students, occasionally helping them to clarify a point, serving as a timekeeper, and generally facilitating the meeting. She prefers to skim through the papers shortly before the group meets, sometimes even waiting until the students start discussing a particular paper to study it in any detail. She does this because it forces her "not to come to the meeting with a head full of ideas about the papers," which, she believes, will encourage her to get too involved. Eileen's basic attitude about peer-group conferences is captured in the way she describes her role: "hands off."

Michael respects the nature of peer conferences as a collaborative activity but cannot understand why some teachers would completely abrogate their responsibility in order to listen to three or four relatively uninformed novices praise each other's flawed efforts. He thinks that students can, with a little guidance, constructively critique each other's writing. In fact, at one of the departmental seminars he even criticized teachers who think that collaboration among students is like "the blind leading the blind." But he believes that the key to students' progress as writers and revisers is the process of modeling. He likes to spend fifteen minutes at the front of the class doing his own critique of a draft to show the students how to do it. As far as peer-group conferences are concerned, he thinks that, as long as he has a captive audience of three or four students, he can take at least some time to demonstrate the processes of active response and revision. Students are not silenced, but neither is he. His philosophy comes, in part, from his previous experiences in work settings, where he noticed again and again how important it was for a writer to have a model to work from.

Eileen's and Michael's students are in the middle of their second paper, an analysis of a social problem. As part of their "research" for this paper, the students have conducted informal interviews with people who have some expertise on the issue. In both sections, the students are practicing integrating outside sources into their papers. In this case, Eileen and Michael think that interview material represents a more productive outside source than library research because the material is more unpolished in its verbal form.

Below are transcriptions of several minutes of one peer-group conference in Eileen's class and one in Michael's class.

Excerpts from Eileen's Group Conference

Deb's paper is being discussed. Several minutes of casual conversation precede the discussion, then:

Eileen: Okay, who do you want to begin with? Who's real eager to go?

Deb: I'll be eager; what the heck! [laughs]

Eileen: Why don't you tell us a little about what you've been doing in this . . .

Deb: Well, I've finally found a problem that I actually like, so it's getting more interesting for me to research on that kind of thing. Talking to that guy was really interesting. [She talks for another 45 seconds about her interview.] Only thing I'm having . . . I need to sort out some of my ideas a little bit more clearly, and I do intend to put more of the interview in the paper, but I'm having a hard time transcribing it and getting it all put together; I still have to work on that a little bit.

Sue: Who'd you interview?

Deb: [She talks for a minute or two about the interviewee, the head of the scholastic conduct committee.]

Eileen: How did you all react to this? What kinds of things did you focus on?

Sue: Uh, in the first paragraph, I wondered why you put "mean euphemism."

Deb: Oh, that's "mere." Did I . . . I probably spelled "mere" wrong [as "mear"].

Sue: M-E-R-E. [laughter] I thought it said "mean."

Eileen: [Laughing] A lot of people don't get their *n*'s right, right? That's a mean euphemism!

Deb: [Laughing harder] I did use my dictionary for "euphemism"! I just forgot to spell "mere" right.

Sue: [Still laughing] Anyway. I thought that when you have this sentence that says how this problem has been able to endure, that seemed kind of long, kind of dragged out. I thought maybe you . . .

Scott: Where's this? First paragraph?

Sue: First paragraph, see where she wrote "how"? I just thought maybe it would be better to say we need to examine the reasons why this problem has been allowed to grow, whereas this seems to be beating around the bush a little, and it's kind of hard to figure out what you're talking about. You know what I mean? And then I didn't think your break was right for your paragraph.

Deb: Where would you break it?

Sue: Maybe the sentence before it? You know, say that that could be . . . the clear definition . . .

Deb: Oh, I see what you're saying. It probably would be better to get that out of the top.

Scott: So you end up with a question and then . . . I said the same thing; I said "maybe a new topic there before the paragraph on the definition": "One possible reason why academic dishonesty is so clouded with misunderstanding is that we don't have an adequate definition for it."

Sue: Right, and then what you have for the first sentence of the next paragraph, it says, a major complaint, and then you tell two complaints, kind of. There's not a clear-cut definition, and the cases are individual. Those are two different things, not one.

Eileen: Where is this, now?

Deb: I think I'm meaning them to be one, but I've worded it strangely.

Scott: The first, where she's got the paragraph marking . . .

Deb: What the complaint is, that because the cases are individual, the clear-cut definition doesn't work. I probably didn't say that. [laughs]

Sue: Okay, because to me it sounds like you've got two ideas, not one.

Eileen: The definition, and the fact that each case is individual?

Scott: Yeah.

Deb: I might even drop that individual thing altogether; it doesn't fit very well. That was just my personal opinion as I was reading through; I don't know.

Scott: But . . . if, I think it's important to have in there because the case may be individual and hard to . . .

Deb: Or maybe provide the case, because the case that I have is really interesting. It was in the interview, so I could stick it in there—it was about the computer student who tossed one of his programs in the wastebasket and someone else pulled it out and used it and they both supposedly failed the course because you're not supposed to have even near identical cases or something in computer land. [The group discusses this incident for another two minutes.] I don't know if that . . .

Scott: Maybe word it differently, you know, and give an example of the case, and after that say that no two cases are ever the same, you know, because . . .

Deb: I don't know. I'll see what I can do.

Scott: Because I think that's an important thing to say, that that's why it's hard to, to define . . .

Deb: To define it, yeah. 'Cause everything's different. [The group pauses, flips through Deb's draft.]

Eileen: Well, what else stood out for you folks—anything you noticed or found interesting or problematic?

Deb: I have a question. Does it bother you that I quoted the whole conduct thing?

Sue: I think it fits nicely.

Deb: Okay, because what I thought is, if I try and paraphrase it, I might screw it up, and it's so technical and it's been reworked and reworked and reworked by the people who sit on this committee. But it was a really long quote and I didn't know if it bothered people or not.

Eileen: You mean the definition of academic dishonesty?

Deb: Yeah. The university's.

Sue: I think it's most effective that way.

Scott: You know what I said, I put in the margin, "But I thought you said that there wasn't any good definition yet?" Up here.

Deb: Okay, I should check that out.

Scott: And then, I'm wondering if you said that there isn't any clear definition. Oh, I guess you're . . .

Deb: For colleges in general.

Scott: So maybe you should make that clear. See, you say first a clear definition is in order . . .

Eileen: Yeah, implying that there isn't a clear definition . . .

Scott: And then we get this pretty complex definition here [the quotation].

Sue: Yeah, it would be hard . . . I mean, I read that thing, and it really blows you away. [pause as the group thinks and rereads]

Eileen: How would you get around that problem? [pause; no response; group reading] How about this . . . what if you took the definition thing out of here and maybe integrate this definition into this whole discussion here. Um . . . "A lot of the way that people talk about and treat academic dishonesty has to do with the definition that they're using. At the university the definition is such-and-such, um, which seems to be pretty adequate for defining it," at least that's what you seem to be saying.

Deb: Um-hmm.

Eileen: But in many other places the definitions are different or there aren't any at all, you know.

Scott: I mean, I know that cheating's a problem. I mean, through all the universities it's a problem. But are you just concentrating on the university?

Deb: I think I'm going to have to limit it to that, because citing a whole bunch of examples, I don't know . . . some of my research has, like, what do other schools do, like in some schools misconduct is chewing gum in class. I mean, [laughs] let's be real, does that even count? [gives more examples, one minute] To throw all that in messes it up.

Sue: I don't know. I mean, doesn't that show the range of . . .

Deb: Of severity?

Eileen: So academic dishonesty is defined in a lot of different ways, all the way from chewing gum to, you know; or it's treated in these different ways; some people have elaborate committees, and other places just leave it up to the teacher or something, I don't know. It might be worth demonstrating the range, and then you get to this thing about how there isn't an adequate definition.

Deb: "An example of this would be . . . that which is implemented by the university." Right. [pause; groups reads]

Sue: Okay, I have, on the second page, where you start your new paragraph about how is it that students don't feel responsible? One thing I didn't like all the questions all at once. I wondered if it wouldn't be better just to work it through and answer the questions along the way . . . [The conference continues for about ten more minutes.]

Excerpts from Michael's Group Conference

The group has just finished discussing Bob's paper. Sam's paper is now going to be discussed.

Michael: Okay. Sam.

Sam: Okay. Well, this is a problem I dealt with in my last paper, and I couldn't find any information on dorm parties and stuff from my interview with my R.A. [resident assistant]. So I took campus drinking as my problem, and I was trying to tie it into the drinking aspect, especially how the drinking affects the grades. And it was tough to connect that with the dorms; I just tried to hint at it, but it didn't seem like it came across too well.

Michael: Maybe it's just not dorm parties that are the problem. Maybe they're not the only cause; it's parties in general, all over the place. If you're talking about 60 percent of the people whose grades go down, 60 percent of the students probably don't even live on campus, so that's not a very good index. That might be two dorm parties compared to ten on campus. So I think you should change the problem so that it's not just dorm parties.

Sam: So it's just . . .

Michael: So it's college students. It's not logical with the information you use. You've got symptoms or byproducts of problems that you're passing off as problems. It's not the dorm parties; those are the symptoms of a larger problem, and that's what you should focus on.

Louise: Or is it the cause of another problem?

Michael: Oh, like peer pressure? I don't know. That's probably wrapped up with the larger problem. So you need to work on this first paragraph where your focus is confused. You need to reorganize this, do some mapping or something.

Bob: Also, there are rules, I mean, in our dorm, you're supposed to have quiet hours, at ten o'clock at night. But they don't enforce the rules; the parties go on until 1:00 a.m. sometimes.

Michael: That might be related to your conclusion. I think you need to make your solutions stronger. You could include this enforcement of policies business as another solution.

Louise: I put down [in her comments] that another solution would be to enforce the noise, you know, how loud you can get, and give them a warning. That might be a good way to enforce the party rules and cut down on drinking.

Michael: Yeah, though I suppose they'll keep on drinking somewhere else. The problem may not be remedied by simply enforcing rules. You need to include some arguments that can't be easily refuted. Again, you're alleviating the symptoms, noisy parties. But are you really getting rid of the cause?

Bob: It's probably not easy to enforce rules because . . .

Michael: And your paper's not very conclusive at the end. You should probably expand on the solutions you have and find some more, and then bring them together at the end. Also, I think your structures, too . . . you need to vary the sentences—your sentences are a lot like the ones Bob has: "The only problem with that is there are. . . ." Change that to "Clearly, however, such rules are difficult to enforce," instead of "the only problem is that there," because you get that "is" verb, and what it does is it makes the prose fall flat on its face. If you can get a powerful verb in there . . . verbs are the life of the language, and if you can have those powerful verbs ... uh, this way you give the sentence the power of the verb "enforce." And then you could have, "Part of the excitement of dorm drinking perhaps originates in the glee of violating university policies," because that's part of it, and that's the point you're making. The stronger the rules, the more fun it is to break them. If our society was ... in fact, that's a big case about drinking in other societies; in some cultures there are no drinking ages at all, and yet they don't have the same kinds of problems for some reason. People don't get together and get their kegs, and ask somebody who's older to buy the stuff and sneak around and all that. It's not as exciting because everyone can do it, you know, you kind of grow up with it. It would be like, if they completely banned semipornographic magazines like *Playboy,* you know, there would be a lot of excitement in trying to get hold of those things. That may be something to do with drinking in the dorms; it's fun to do partly because of the risk.

Louise: I said the sentences aren't real precise and kind of wander.

Michael: Right. Look at your sentences and revise them to make them smoother and more stylish. There are some kind of choppy parts of the essay. So you need to work on sentences, organization, and finding some more solutions to the problem, or looking at the problem and thinking about whether it's a problem or just symptoms of something larger, you know, some social or cultural thing. [The conference continues in this way for another five minutes.]

ISSUES FOR DISCUSSION

• How would you characterize the way each teacher runs his or her peer-group conferences? What, specifically, leads you to that characterization?

• What are the strengths and weaknesses of each teacher's facilitative style?

• If you were a student, which conference would you rather be in? Why?

• Which conference do you think is more productive—that is, in which one do you think students learn more effectively about writing? Why?

• What's the most appropriate role for a teacher in a peer-group conference? Why?

• Are students really capable of giving each other useful advice about their writing? If this advice is usually not as useful as the teacher's advice, are collaborative activities overrated and overused?

• What issues of power, control, and classroom management are raised by the two transcriptions? Is either teacher too "wimpy"? Is either teacher too "dominant" and appropriative?

• If you were in a discussion group with Eileen and Michael after several of you had tape-recorded your conferences, what suggestions would you give them for their own practices? On what basis?

Trevor's Journal

Jan Barrymore is teaching freshman composition and has decided to use journals in her course. The journals are designed to serve two main purposes: first, to be a repository for ideas, musings, drafts, and other "in-process" material for the main assignments in the course; second, to provide a context for the students' reactions to readings and more general thoughts about writing. Jan has described the journals as generally academic: although she does not disallow personal reflections or "diary-like" entries, she has made it clear that she would rather that students focus on the material of the course when they do their self-sponsored writing. For Jan, this emphasis on the academic side of journal writing comes from her dissatisfaction with the sort of material she has seen in the usually more reflective, personal journals she has asked students to keep in the past. That material has seemed fairly "soft" intellectually and does not, in Jan's mind, contribute much to students' learning in light of the time it takes them to write.

Jan has asked the students to write frequently in their journals, which she will grade at the end of the course mainly in terms of the quantity of acceptable journal writing. Along the way, she will collect single entries every week or so, responding to them marginally and returning them to the students ungraded. She has promised to provide feedback on the students' ideas, but is wary of taking on an unreasonable load.

The course has been in session for one week. The class is reading several short, personal essays in which the authors recount experiences that made them reflect on important political, social, and environmental issues: the "ant" scene in Thoreau's *Walden;* "At the Dam," Joan Didion's tiny vignette about her visit to the Hoover Dam; Langston Hughes's memory of "being saved" in "Salvation"; and Madelon Sprengnether's "Los Alamos," in which the author expresses her views of nuclear weapons while on a visit to New Mexico. In addition to the new perspectives offered in these essays, Jan hopes to use them to show her students how personal experiences can lead to a form of "narrative exposition" that can address content traditionally associated with "argumentative" or "expository" essays. After reading and discussing the essays, the students will begin their own writing projects in a similar vein.

For the first of her regular journal assignments, Jan has also asked the class to choose one of the four readings and to reflect on or react to it informally in a page or two. She will collect the entries, respond briefly to them, check them for credit, and return them to the students for reinsertion into their notebooks.

Trevor Harris, one student in the class, has already been quite outspoken, challenging some of the ideas in Jan's syllabus and even, on one occasion, interrupting her to point out that she had scheduled a class session during a school holiday. While Trevor seems to Jan quite articulate, she already worries that his highly conservative views and dominant, almost brash class demeanor spell trouble.

At the end of class on the day the first journal entries are due, Trevor dutifully hands his paper to Jan while leaving the room, but, just as she takes it, he says, "Hope you like it. I had lots of fun trashing this lady's bleeding-heart liberalism; what a joke." Then he saunters out with the other students.

Jan is surprised, on looking at Trevor's journal entry, to find a neatly typed, rather formal discussion of Sprengnether's essay,[1] since Jan made it quite clear that the journals could be messy, exploratory, and informal—a place for students to try out ideas and question themselves, not argue or persuade.

Here is Trevor's journal entry:

> Trevor Harris: Journal
> Entry #1
> April 03
> Review of "Los Alamos" by Madelon Sprengnether
>
> This essay describes the authors view of nuclear weapon technology and her experiences while visiting Los Alamos, New Mexico. She is opposed to the use and development of nuclear weapon technology. Her views are ridiculously liberal and very contradictory to what is real in life. I will examine three examples from her text.
>
> She compares the erruption of a volcano with the destruction caused by nuclear weapons. She then implies that because of the devestation caused they are "bad." In this examples we first see her naivete. The two are very different. Not because of what they do, but because of why they occured. A volcanic eruption is a natural disaster and lies outside the realm of human control. Because of this, it is an unfortunate occurance. The destruction of Hiroshima and Nagasaki in Japan were within the realm of human control. There was great destruction, however it was the Jappanese that brought it

upon themselves. It was unfortunate that the Jappanese people did not have enough intelligence to make moral decisions in their international affairs. It was not unfortunate that they were destroyed. That is what they chose. If we were to show pity for everyone who made poor decisions, we would do nothing else.

She makes the comment that those involved in making the first atomic bomb showed more concern over their accomplishment than what devestation they caused. Again she is saying that something is wrong, when it is not. The people involved in the research have every right to be proud of what they did. They put a lot of effort into developing a new major war technology. This technology was able to assist the Nation in wining a major war as well as to have far reaching implications in other technologies as well. Nuclear technology can be used in the production of electricity and in various medical procedures. There was so much to be gained from their research, and so little to loose. The destruction of those who deserved to be destroyed can not be considered a loss. They died, but we thrive.

She also comments on the history of American Indians in the area. She makes the statement "There is no place on this continent where a European descendant can feel blameless." What is there to blame them? At that time in our history, and in the history of the world in general, the acquisition of new territory for settlement was a fundamental right of the people. We took land that was rightfully ours. The Indians were resettled. It is not like we simply fruitlessly slaughtered all of them, just killed the ones who resisted our rightful settlement. It was the standard of the time. Even if the standards have changed, one should not be compelled to feel responsible for something that was, in all regards, the right thing to do.

In closing she states she expresses her concerns because she is "head over heels in love with this earth." What she proposes is stagnation and the vaccation of the fundamentals of this great Nation. As a nation we are commpelled to success, to survive is not enough. To stand by and allow our way of life to be threatened by other nations or even destroyed would be foolish, to say the least. Secondly, if she is truly in love with this earth, why does she strive for its stagnattion? The earth is full of change. The world is dynamic. Some things will forever disappear, like Indians, Japanese cities, and so forth, so that other things can be made to appear. If she is looking for divine purpose, how does she know what it is?

ISSUES FOR DISCUSSION

- How would you respond to this journal entry?

- Trevor's writing is more formal than Jan expects in the students' journals. Should she discourage such formal writing? Why or why not?

- Trevor's ideas are well expressed but reveal several problems, both in logic and, more subjectively, in their underlying ethic. Should Jan point out Trevor's flaws in reasoning, and if so, to what end? Should she compel Trevor to question his ideology? Why or why not?

- Jan has promised to respond to the entries she collects. What form should her response take? Is it acceptable for her not to respond at all to Trevor's entry?

- What effect, if any, should Jan's knowledge of Trevor's classroom demeanor or expressed political position have on her response?

- While Jan's journal assignments are supposed to be fairly "academic," she has also encouraged students to express their own ideas freely. Should she reward, with positive comments, Trevor's free expression in the journal entry? Will raising opposition to Trevor's ideas set a more constrained context for further journal writing?

- Jan's personal response to Trevor's entry is anger bordering on outrage. She feels a moral responsibility to change Trevor's views. What advice would you give her about coming to terms with her feelings? Would you caution her to suppress her emotions in responding to Trevor? Why or why not?

Responding to the Unexpected

For the first essay in her freshman composition course, Mary Albera wanted her students to reflect on events that lead people to feel transformed. She assigned two outside readings as a means of generating ideas—Langston Hughes's "Salvation" and E. B. White's "Once More to the Lake." By organizing the students into discussion groups, she was trying to create an environment in which the students could feel confident expressing their own views about the readings and sharing their own experiences.

One student, Dwayne Lambert, began to draw Mary's attention. He was quite outspoken in class, but not in an inappropriate manner. He had seen Mary on campus occasionally and often behaved with a degree of familiarity she felt less appropriate for a student-teacher relationship than for a student-student relationship. For example, he asked her to join him for coffee (she always refused), and he suggested good nightclubs. Once he asked Mary how old she was, and when she answered, he made a comment about how close they were in age. Mary became apprehensive about how he might behave in class. However, he was one of the more talkative and hardworking students. In fact,

he often impressed other members of the class with his ability to take
on a viewpoint and defend it well. During the discussion of "Salvation,"
for instance, he insisted that, unlike Hughes's narrator, he would not
have given in to the pressures of the congregation, but would have
remained firm in the "truth" of the absence of any religious experience.
He persuasively argued that falsely representing oneself is dishonest
and more immoral than the failure to experience a religious conversion
at a young age.

Mary's assignment asked the students to recall some childhood
experience or event, then write a narrative that communicated the
effect or realization caused by the experience. Most students turned in
interesting accounts of their past experiences, using aspects of the
assigned readings to help them relate their own ideas more clearly.

When she reached Dwayne's draft, however, Mary was troubled.
Although it was clearly rendered in narrative form, Dwayne's experience
seemed almost unbelievable and contained subject matter that chal-
lenged Mary's authority. His essay consisted of a "story" in which a
high school boy's new, young Spanish teacher (the same age as Mary)
seduces him, and they have an affair. Romantic scenes were described
in detail, although the characters were not likable or sympathetic.
Rather, they seemed one-dimensional and unrealistic, confirming Mary's
suspicion that the event had never happened. The essay was mechan-
ically correct, and the sentences were syntactically varied, but beneath
the correctness lay a situation that seemed constructed from a desire
to seduce the instructor. Mary felt, personally and professionally, as
though she were being "tested" by Dwayne. She was offended both by
the generally insulting attitude of the essay towards women and by the
personal nature of the narrative.

ISSUES FOR DISCUSSION

• How should Mary respond to Dwayne's essay: in written comments
on the essay itself? in conference?

• Should her comments address the personal nature of the essay in
any way? Will any admission that she has taken the essay personally
increase the problem or create future difficulty in handling this student?

• Dwayne's essay obviously has not fulfilled the purpose of the
assignment, which was to narrate an actual experience in an interesting
and revelatory way. Ought Mary to challenge the truth of Dwayne's
narrative? How might he react?

• Should Mary's personal opinions about this student and his forwardness affect her comments on his writing? Will she be able to treat his writing fairly and objectively? Should she be expected to do so?

• Would it be appropriate not to accept the essay, even though it is as well written, technically, as many other students' essays?

• Should Mary do anything in class to alter teacher-student distance? What are some particular actions she might take? How might she handle future classes in order to establish a rapport which might best prevent the repetition of this type of experience?

A Problem of Ethics

Betsy Roche had been teaching the second of her university's required writing courses for three terms, and she felt as though she was really getting the hang of it. The university's description of the course, "The Research Paper," stipulated that it "introduce the students to principles and methods of conducting research and require them to produce 15 to 18 pages of research-based prose." In the hands of the wrong teacher, the course could be deadly: an entire term of getting to know your way around the library, talking about narrowing your topic and writing a thesis statement, practicing skills like paraphrasing and quoting, and going over a dozen possible entry formats in a works cited list. Necessary stuff for a college student, but scut work.

The good teachers on the staff, though, did a great job with the course, and Betsy was among the best. These teachers did not see it simply as instruction, drill, and practice of research-paper skills; instead, they saw the course as the opportunity to have their students participate in a sustained intellectual exercise on a single, challenging topic for an entire term. Instead of focusing initially on the skills that students should learn, these instructors focused from the beginning on the intellectual endeavor the entire class was participating in, and then they taught the research-paper skills as tools the students would need to report the research—the new knowledge—they were discovering. Thus it became a course in academic argument, examining how scholars in different fields construct their versions of the "truth," how they aim to get readers to accept their theses, how they employ the rhetoric of their disciplines. The course was a challenge for students and gained the reputation as being "tough but worth the effort" along the campus grapevine.

These courses generally examined one specific topic. One section looked at "The History of Rock 'n' Roll" in a stimulating, academic way. Another examined "Childhood Psychology and Children's Poetry."

Yet another worked with "You Are What You Eat: Nutrition and Health."

Betsy's focus was a bit broader—she called her course "Ethical Issues for the Nineties." Betsy liked teaching the course because it allowed her to translate an important part of her personal world into her professional life. A doctoral student specializing in Old English, she spent most of her time studying difficult ancient European languages and obscure poems and sagas. Unlike some of her graduate student colleagues, who were studying rhetoric and composition, or creative writing, or even more modern periods of literature, she found that very little of her own course work had any bearing on the writing courses she taught. To be sure, she could occasionally amuse the students with anecdotes about the etymology of some terms they came across, but that was about the extent of her "relevance."

Her personal life was another matter, however. Betsy was very active in the young adults' group of the large city church she attended. For that group, she had organized a literacy tutoring program in which young, urban professionals volunteered their time with children and adults from the nearby public housing projects. She worked with one of the clergy in a citywide effort to provide more single-resident occupancy hotels for homeless men and women. And she volunteered two nights a month as a counselor in a hospice run by the university hospital. In addition, Betsy was a longstanding member of her state's chapter of the National Organization for Women and had worked in two statewide political campaigns for candidates who supported pro-choice and women's rights legislation. When it came to considering contemporary ethical issues, Betsy was both opinionated and extremely well informed.

Her reading list for "Ethical Issues" was quite stimulating. In addition to having her students study a brief manual on conducting and reporting research, she required them to read (all in the first three weeks of the semester) a monograph-length introduction to moral philosophy by James Rachels and excerpts from three contemporary treatises on ethics: Alasdair MacIntyre's *After Virtue,* Robert Bellah and associates' *Habits of the Heart,* and Barbara Ehrenreich's *Fear of Falling.* After providing this theoretical grounding, she set out casebooks of readings on three issues—euthanasia, marriage and divorce, and public housing—and required the students to select one of these as the general area for their first paper. Each student developed an arguable thesis and wrote a five- to seven-page paper, using the materials Betsy provided. The pedagogy worked: by midterm, the students had produced very interesting, well-written papers.

During the remaining weeks, the students were to produce a final, longer paper on an ethical issue of their choice, and Betsy had developed an effective strategy for getting this paper started. She asked the students to produce a one-page proposal in which they would introduce the ethical issue they planned to write about, explain what they knew about this issue already, and pose at least two questions about the topic that might focus their research efforts, at least initially. In her previous sections, this proposal had allowed Betsy to intervene in the students' research and writing process right from the beginning, to advise them about sources they might consult, to hint about theses that had been overworked to the point of being clichéd, and to suggest fresh approaches to the topics. In her comment on the proposal, Betsy would either approve the project or suggest a revision of the research plan.

Most in the class appreciated this opportunity to get the instructor's input, but three students dragged their feet on getting the proposal in. The day before it was due, they came to see Betsy in her office and told her, in so many words, that they felt they were being required to commit themselves to a topic too early. They wondered why they could not simply do some more reading and thinking for a couple of weeks and then write a paper about "something that's really interesting, not all this boring stuff." Betsy was suspicious. None of them was a particularly good student, and she suspected that they might want a couple of weeks to check various campus files for finished papers that they could doctor up a bit and hand in as their own.

What's more, for the past month or so she had been feeling a kind of animosity growing between herself and James Addickes, the student who was doing most of the talking for this gang of three. It had begun in the class discussion of the Ehrenreich excerpt and had grown to palpable proportions when the class considered together some issues surrounding public housing. When James offered in class that public housing was nothing more than a way to "allow pimps, prostitutes, and junkies to live on the dole and avoid getting a job," Betsy restrained her inclination to snap at him. Instead, she patiently offered some documented resources about the positive correlations between public housing and employability, and she put her anger on the back burner. The other two students had not exactly rubbed her the wrong way, but neither had they done anything to distinguish themselves, and their association with James in this matter did not improve their standing with her.

She said no to their request—she had to have a proposal from them by the next day. If they wanted to change their topic later on, she told them, they would have to submit another proposal and a written explanation of their reasons for wanting to change it. The other two were silent, but James spoke up as he was leaving: "Okay, have it your way. I'll shoot from the hip." Betsy closed the office and went home in a foul humor.

The next day, all three were absent from class. Betsy made note of this fact and proceeded to collect the proposals and teach a session on getting started on the longer paper. With five minutes remaining in the class, James sauntered in and sat down. When the bell rang, he walked up and handed a proposal to Betsy. She asked him where his two partners were. "Don't know," he said. "It wasn't my turn to babysit them today." He smiled and walked out. Betsy filed his proposal with the others and wished that she had never met James Addickes.

She had blocked out two hours in her library carrel immediately after class to read the proposals so that she could return them on Monday. She knew she did not want to read James's first because she was still so incensed, so she buried his proposal in the stack of twenty-three and got started. Most of them were great: the students were interested in issues ranging from welfare mothers to job training for convicted felons to government subsidies for the tobacco industry. She was able to approve these projects, offer starting points for their readings, and refine many of their questions.

About an hour into the reading, she got to James's proposal. She resisted her temptation to put it off until last—"might as well stick the thorn in the middle of the roses," she thought—and began to read. This was his proposal:

James Addickes
Ms. Roche, instructor
THE CRIME OF ABORTION: A PROPOSAL
I propose to write my research paper about the crime of abortion. What I know already is this: Millions of unborn babies are killed every year just because their mothers were promiscuous and didn't bother to use birth control, and these babies aren't in any position to defend themselves from this slaughter. My two questions:
1. Can government officials bring charges of murder against women who have abortions?
2. Should state governments require a written consent form from the fathers of these unborn children before permitting women to have an abortion?

Betsy couldn't believe it. Her many years of soul-searching and active campaigning for the pro-choice movement, and her two years of working with students as they wrote about sensitive ethical issues, all seemed to have come to this: she saw James's proposal as a little puddle of acid eating away at her life and principles. What could she possibly say in response? She composed herself as best she could and wrote this note on the proposal:

> *James:*
>
> *After our little disagreement yesterday about the proposal deadline, I had hoped that our difficulties might be behind us. But this proposal troubles me immensely. First of all, you oper- ate on several assumptions that most people simply don't ac- cept: that women have abortions only because they have been promiscuous—that they have been "bad girls" and had sex without "protecting themselves," that the fetuses that are aborted are viable human entities, that men should have the ultimate say over what happens to women's bodies, just to name three. As a first step, let me suggest that you read the history of the Roe versus Wade Supreme Court decision. I can provide you with some literature in class on Monday. As a second step, let me urge you strongly to think about writing your paper on another topic. Given the nature of our relation- ship, and given my strong feelings on women's rights in the pro-choice movement, I really don't see how I could participate in any discussions of this topic with you, nor do I see how I could possibly evaluate your work fairly. Please see me after class on Monday.*

Betsy read through the rest of the proposals and called it quits. She knew she probably had not heard the last of James Addickes, but she did not want him to ruin her weekend. She would deal with him next week.

On Monday, she returned the proposals and spent most of the hour commenting on general strategies about refining research questions, using the students' work as examples. She did not mention James's proposal, but she did announce that she was going directly to her office, so if any students wanted immediate feedback, they should see her right after class.

James had not said a word in class, but about fifteen minutes after she got settled in her office, he showed up at the door. He did not come in; he simply stood in the doorway. "Are you saying you can't grade me fairly because we believe different things about abortion?" he blurted out. "Well, I suppose yes, in part, but I wouldn't exactly put it that way," Betsy replied. "That's all I wanted to know," James shot back, and he left abruptly. No one else showed up during the office hour, and Betsy went home greatly perturbed.

When she arrived at her departmental mailbox the next day, Betsy found a note from the department chair, who needed to see her immediately. Needless to say, she felt a twinge of apprehension as she headed to the departmental office. The chair saw her coming and immediately steered her into his office. "We've got big trouble," he sputtered. "You've got some kid named James Addickes in your research-paper class, right?" Betsy nodded, wondering what further havoc James could wreak. "Well, I just talked to the chancellor's secretary on the phone. It seems that Addickes's father—he's a lawyer downtown—has already been on the phone with the chancellor and the dean this morning. Seems that he intends to sue you, me, the college, and university for violating his son's first-amendment right to freedom of speech. I don't know what this guy's agenda is, but we've got to work fast to head off this problem."

ISSUES FOR DISCUSSION

• Should Betsy have seen the trouble with James coming long before the disagreement over the proposal? In the discussion concerning public housing, for example, was Betsy right to curb her anger and not say anything to James? How might she have reacted differently in the class? in the conference?

• How do you think Betsy handled the disagreement over the proposal? What might she have done differently? What especially do you think of the comment she wrote? Does it incriminate her in any way? What would you have written?

• If this situation happened on your own campus, who might a teaching assistant or faculty member turn to in order to assure that his or her legal rights and best interests were protected?

• In general, what do you think of having students read, discuss, and write about "controversial" topics in college writing courses? Is there any way to do so without opening yourself to problems such as the ones Betsy encountered?

The Prince

Marty Corden was teaching the argumentation section of a special-topic composition course, "Writing about War." To introduce a reading assignment on Machiavelli's *The Prince,* Marty helped the class understand the way arguments have traditionally been constructed, with thesis, premise, body paragraphs, and refutation. Working through a college writing handbook, the class examined strong and weak thesis statements, tested premises, and wrote outlines for a number of arguments.

As a preview, the students read the first page of *The Prince.* Marty emphasized that they should consider Machiavelli's general argument and should avoid becoming tied down by the historical examples Machiavelli provides to support his claims. The students were advised to consider Machiavelli's argument concerning the nature and practice of war and to avoid, unless interested in Renaissance history, the intricacies of Florentine politics in Machiavelli's day. The aim of this warning was not to close off avenues of possible research, but rather to reassure the students that no prior knowledge of Renaissance history and culture was necessary to understand the construction of the arguments.

During the time when the students were discussing their own arguments about war and studying the traditional construction of arguments, Marty observed that some students had difficulty understanding the difference between the premises of an argument and its thesis. In a class discussion, some were reasoning from concepts related to cultural premises about masculinity and femininity, and others were reasoning from concepts about the individual as a unity and as a series of roles.

One student able to perceive the premises coloring her claims was Rhonda Davis, a creative thinker who attended class regularly, contributed to class discussion on reading assignments and rough drafts, and came to conferences with serious questions about her own writing responses to reading assignments. She had expressed an interest in writing short fiction and had already taken and completed a creative writing workshop course. Rhonda appeared to have no difficulty mastering the art of argumentation and had made a number of astute remarks suggesting the deficiencies in the examples of weak thesis statements studied in class.

Rhonda also seemed to grasp the construction of arguments in another work assigned as a way of introducing *The Prince,* the short article by Adrienne Rich entitled "Vietnam and Sexual Violence." The class had discussed this article and then summarized the major points of Rich's argument by going through the article paragraph by paragraph, with the class calling out each paragraph's main point, which was then written on the board. Rhonda participated by not only stating the main point of the paragraph in question, but also by offering her response to the premises on which Rich's argument is founded.

For his first specific assignment on *The Prince,* Marty asked the class to summarize one chapter and to comment briefly on the rhetorical construction of the chosen section. Rhonda had little difficulty completing this exercise, although Marty noticed that this paper seemed less polished than her previous work. For the next assignment, he asked the students to take a brief quotation from Machiavelli and to write a short argumentative paper on a thesis suggested by the passage.

The week before the assignment was due, Rhonda was unexpectedly absent from class. She had also missed her conference on her preliminary draft as well as the class review of second drafts, and she was absent on the day the essay was due. When she submitted the essay three days after the deadline, she put it into Marty's mailbox rather than bringing it to class. The other students had selected their quotations wisely and argued their premises persuasively. Rhonda, however, made no attempt to construct a line of reasoning to support her claim that Machiavelli was right in saying that people can be easily deceived by a wily deceiver. Instead, she described her own dismay over the way a man she loved had deceived her by breaking his promise that he would not confide in others about her personal affairs. Even as a personal essay, the writing was weak because it lacked vividness and a clear narrative frame. Rhonda concluded by stating that no one can be trusted, a sweeping generalization unlike the kinds of multivalent claims she had been making in earlier class discussions and in earlier essays.

ISSUES FOR DISCUSSION

• When Marty introduces a reading assignment, should he emphasize his role as (1) a facilitator of personal responses to the general topic of a reading; (2) a guide through such generic-discursive formations as arguments; (3) or a provider of opportunities for drawing students' attention to the premises, or ideologies, in the arguments?

• Should Marty accept the essay but give it a low grade since (1) it was late; (2) it lacked sufficient proof for, as well as reasoning about, the claim that Machiavelli's quotation on deceivers is true; (3) it "tells" rather than "shows" Rhonda's deceiving friend and her reactions to him? Should he give positive comments about Rhonda's independence in developing her response? Should he indicate his uneasiness over the possible consequences for her if she were to continue opposing tasks assigned in other disciplines or other writing situations with tasks she sets for herself?

Note

1. The article to which Trevor responded was an early, unrevised draft of Madelon Sprengnether's "Los Alamos 1987" (*Great River Review,* forthcoming), which the instructor used in class with the author's permission. The content and quotations in Trevor's entry do not accurately reflect Sprengnether's published essay.

4 Teaching "Grammar," Usage, and Style in Context

Grammar—the dreaded word! Try asking a random sample of people on the street how they would define *good writing*. Don't be surprised if many of them answer, "Good grammar, and correct spelling." In fact, when you go out socially with a group of nonacademics, and you tell them that you teach writing, the first reaction of most of them will probably be a chagrined admission: "I was a terrible writer in school. My grammar was awful!"

Most teachers of writing feel pulled in two directions about grammar. On the one hand, they learn about the subtleties of persuasion, rhetorical contexts, and cognitive strategies that the discipline of composition studies has come to comprise. On the other hand, they are confronted with institutional expectations (perhaps in the form of exit exams or minimum competency exams) and with student papers that demand attention to what can loosely be characterized as language problems.

Students get a mixed message from their teachers about language problems. First, most students have probably had an English teacher who commented immediately (and perhaps voluminously and vociferously) on their errors. When this happens, students easily come to believe that what matters *most* is avoiding errors: whatever they do to write good ideas that are well developed and organized, whatever they do to structure sentences well and use effective diction, is not as important to the teacher, they think, as avoiding mistakes. But in their assessments, most writing teachers *do* focus on quality, organization, and development of ideas, as well as sentence maturity, style, and diction, more sharply than on correct spelling, grammar, mechanics, and punctuation.

But how can teachers convince students that we *really* believe in these priorities? How do we convince them, in other words, that even though correctness may not be the *most* important feature of their writing, it is still extremely important?

The sample cases in this chapter focus on various language problems common in the teaching of writing. Very likely, discussion of these cases will move from the more obvious questions of correctness to the more subtle questions of how a teacher corrects without stifling, suggests

63

without deprecating, and remediates without robbing the text of the student's voice or meaning.

Where Do You Start?

Mollie O'Rourke, who is in her fifth year as a writing instructor, has at least three things in common with many of her colleagues. First, in responding to and evaluating student writing, she tries to put as much responsibility for revision and improvement as possible on the student writers themselves—Mollie will not rewrite her students' papers for them. Second, she constructs every writing assignment so that the students, if they choose to, will be able to submit a first draft both to her and their peers for commentary to be used in planning revisions. Third, because she believes that students in college writing courses should be able to write intelligently about important current affairs, she often develops writing assignments that enable her students to take positions on issues they encounter in the media.

In March of 1991, Mollie was teaching a general, introductory college writing course. So far in the term, her students had written and revised two essays, both based on readings in their textbook and their own experiences. For the third assignment, Mollie showed the class three examples, taken from popular magazines and newspapers, of the genre known as "news analysis." The students were to use these examples as their models and write an analysis of some feature of the Persian Gulf War.

One student, Roderick Bell, had missed class the day Mollie had set aside for peer-group commentary. The students brought two copies of their rough drafts to class on these days. On one copy, they got comments and suggestions for revision from their classmates. At the end of the day, the students gave the other copy to Mollie so that she could add her suggestions for revision. Even though Roderick missed out on commentary from his peers and his teacher, he did hand in the essay that follows, entitled "The Media," on the day the final draft was due. Mollie was kind-hearted: she decided that rather than grade the piece, she would simply insist that Roderick rewrite it.

Roderick's paper follows.

The Media

News is very important in this country. I for one use to trust the media to report all the information. The overwhelming media in this country is not trustable on its information of the persian gulf war. The medias reports are coflicting when compared to international reports.

The media in the United States is reporting information that is very diffrent from information presented in other countries. The media in the U.S.A. reported by the second week into the war, that the Allied forces suffered little if no losses. The U.S. media also said due to surgical bombing targeted only at military instalations very little civilian injury occured in Iraq. Iraqi news said two 200,000 bed hospitals were filled with injured people. Iranian news reported at least 200,000 were killed or hurt during allied bombing. Pakistany news reported Allied air forces were bombing the city. Another news report conflict is in the phase of war the allied forces are in. A good friend of mine in the army said the ground attack started during the third day of the war, yet we in the U.S.A. were told by the second week the ground war has not begun. The media showed very little Allied cassualty. The media in the U.S. reported by week-2 of the war the U.S. had only lost nine air crafts. At this time Iraqi news said its shot down 180 fighters. CNN reported at least 180 Allied aircraft were lost. A british fighter pillot was intervied after a bombing run. The fighter pillot said, "Iraqi air deffences are like an iron fist." The U.S. news agency reported the U.S. fighters said there was no resistance. A friend of mine in india said, "The Iraqi forces are doing good, they have shot down 137 Allied fighters." I said, "Who told you that?" He said, "Our news agency here reported that." The reports by news agencies other than U.S. had minor differences. In comparison the U.S. reports were far different.

The media reports from other sources are very different from the reports by the U.S. media. Therefore the news media in the U.S. can not be trusted on the situation in the persian gulf.

ISSUES FOR DISCUSSION

• What are your impressions of this paper as a whole? What would you write, both positive and negative, at the end of this paper to guide the revision?

• In light of the mixed messages students might receive if a teacher were to insist that they first correct the obvious grammatical problems in a paper such as this one, how much attention to such errors is appropriate?

• Assuming that pointing out *all* Roderick's errors would lead to cognitive overload—he simply would not be able to process all the problems and would give up in frustration—list *in order of importance* three "grammar"-level features of this piece that you believe he should attend to in his revision.

• What issues in Roderick's paper might you want to bring up with the whole class in large-group discussion or lecture? Which issues do you think would be more appropriate for an individual conference? Why?

The Good Family

Most large universities have a number of students who speak and write English as a second language. These students pose a special challenge to writing teachers. Eric Franzik has taught ESL freshman English for two semesters and has developed a thoroughly multicultural reading list for this class. His goal is to encourage students to become fluent in standard written English while valuing their own and others' cultural diversity. The students in this semester's class were asked to respond to definitions of a "good family" based on mainstream American culture. First, they read Jane Howard's essay on "Families," which describes both biological family units and nonbiological family units such as church groups and friends. In a straightforward way, the essay lists ten characteristics of good families. Eric gave his students the choice of writing a definition modeled after the ten characteristics, or of writing a narrative that illustrated rather than reported on the aspects of a good family. The goal was to have them write an extended definition of a "good family" in their own particular cultures.

Nahomae Teklemarian wrote the following essay for Eric's class:

Good Family

It was in 1980, when my father was acused of helping the Eritrean Peole Liberation Front who were fighting the Ethiopian government. He was jailed without proof and because we were Eritrean. At this time my mother and my father decided that we get out of the city and to go to the north were our grandparent live and to which we are from. And after that to scape from Ethiopia and to go to the country called Sudan which is located in the west of Ethiopia.

After we scape Ethiopia living my father behind, my mother was working hard in order to support me and to my younger sister. Because she paid a lot of money for us in order to get out of Ethiopia, she use to work up to 10 to 15 hours a day in order to pay the rent and other necessary things.

Journey to Sudan was the worst thing that I have experienced. Because we were walking at night so that we can hide from the Ethiopian soldier. It was a cold month and my mother was very worried about us not to get cold and malaria. She used to get up in the morning and cook a meal for us while every body is sleeping and resting.

When we got in Sudan border, my mother had to pay another money so that we can cross the border without being checked by police. After we got to the capital city of Sudan called Khartoum, my mother had to find a place were we can stay. She found her aunt who were living there for ten years. We went to my mother's aunt's place. She gave us a one bedroom from her three bedroom apartment.

After living there for one month, my mother found a house keeping job at the local hotel. That's were she works for ten to fifteen hours for six days. Every time when she come back from work, she brings us fruit and some kind of groceries. She worked for a year and a half very hard in order to feed us.

After working for a year and a half, she applied for a a refugee visa at the United State Embassy. Nine month later, the United State Embassy approved our application and sent a later to my mother saying that "congratulation you and your children will leave to the United State next month." We were so happy jumping all around specially my mother was very happy, she had a tears in her eyes. She wants us to live very happy and to be brave when we get to the United State, because there was a lot of problem that we were going to face. The main problem was that we were a foreign people in a strange land that is far away from our home. And since we were black and does not know the language very well, we did not know how to have a friend and how to progress in life. But that fear is out and behind us now. I thank you my mother for her courage and motivation that brought us the light of freedom. I believe that I have a good family because without them I wouldn't be here living happily in the land I thought strange.

ISSUES FOR DISCUSSION

• What are your impressions of this paper as a whole? As a writing teacher, what specific skills would you want to address in this paper?

• How would you preserve the student's voice while addressing the very real problems of standard written English?

• Should your personal reaction to the content of this essay affect the way you respond to its language problems? Should your knowledge that the student is a non-native speaker affect your response to its language problems?

• What do you see as the differences in language problems between this essay and Roderick's essay in the first scenario?

• What issues in Nahomae's paper might you want to bring up with the whole class in large-group discussion or lecture? Which issues do you think would be more appropriate for an individual conference? Why?

An Abstract Problem

Sandy McAllister, an instructor of advanced composition, had asked the students in her class to find professional or academic journals in their majors, read an article, and write a summary abstract. The assignment had several objectives.

First, Sandy did not assume that, just because the students were juniors and seniors in college, they had ever actually sought out academic journals in the library. So, to begin with, the exercise was a hide-and-seek game—where exactly would they find these professional journals and how would they recognize them?

The second goal for this assignment was reading-related. Could the students read and comprehend the "academic discourse" typical of their own majors, or were they still limited to the textbook-level discourse that characterized their first two years at the university?

Finally, the assignment asked the students to produce a very specific type of academic discourse, the abstract, which required them to try on the "language" of the professionals—the diction, the style, the jargon—in a self-conscious way. The abstracts that follow were written by two students in Sandy's class.

The first student writer, Kim Wilcox, is a hard-working, senior journalism major who is interested in public relations. Although it was not required, she turned in this draft of the abstract for Sandy to evaluate before handing in her final copy.

Why Licensing Won't Work For Public Relations
By Philip Lesly
Summary Abstract

The negative consequences of mandating licensing for public relations are argued and stated in this article.

Licensing in public relations is a invitation for governmental and bureaucratic control of the very liberal field. Licensing would also restrict career mobility and create extreme competition between applicants setting up an expectance of behaviors which would keep many qualified people out. It would also set up boundaries between other professionals in the communication field. People may also limit their education in public relations due to narrower views caused by pressures to pass licensing examinations.

Obstacles could also arise making licensing difficult. This would also mean that any licensing law would have difficulty defining what is and is not allowed in the extremely diverse and variated field. A standard of practice must also be set on the not yet agreed definition of public relations. If a licensing act is passed, bureaucracies would have a hard time controlling the fields' unpredictable nature. The question of who enforces the codes would also be raised creating a struggle of power between bureaucrats and politicians to control the field.

Licensing of public relations could only produce more negative than positive effects. Practitioners who would like to see the field more respected and recognized should generate more regards and consent among themselves, increase own knowledge of the field through literture, and build a solid educational background.

The second student writer, Stanley Brecke, is a computer science major who, in addition to taking advanced composition, is currently enrolled in an independent study course which requires designing, constructing, and testing a multilimbed walking robot to be entered in a national competition. Stanley is an excellent student, clearly comfortable in the discourse of the journals in his field. This assignment posed less of a challenge to him because he has spent a great deal of time reading and interpreting the language of the experts in his field. He wrote this abstract in response to the same assignment that Kim had, but handed in only this required final version:

"The C Language: Key to Portability"
By Edward M. Rifkin and Steve Williams
Computer Design, August 1983

Software compatibility between systems is a major obstacle for the computer designer. This article evaluates whether this compatibility is more easily achieved through a machine independent compiler and a system function library than a universal operating system. It also explains that a C compiler is the probable key to software portability because it is not tied to any one operating system. By using this compiler, and an extensive run-time library, the problems of I/O and high level operations compatibility are easily relieved. In addition, because it is a compact language, C programs are easy to write and debug.

ISSUES FOR DISCUSSION

• What are your impressions of these two abstracts?

• Can you distinguish different kinds of errors in Kim's paper? What do you suppose caused these errors? How would you deal with them?

• Kim has handed in her paper as a "draft" for Sandy to look over before she revises it. None of the other students in the class turned in an abstract for the teacher to "preread." Should Kim be rewarded for her conscientiousness or should she be discouraged from usurping too much of the teacher's attention?

• Sandy has an unexpected difficulty with Stanley's abstract. Since she is not an expert reader of this material, she does not know how to evaluate the language that Stanley uses here ("machine-independent compiler," "extensive run-time library," "compact language," etc.). As a writing teacher, how would you respond to the language of this abstract? How can you critique a passage or a paper if it contains phrases and sentences that you do not understand?

• What issues in Kim's and Stanley's papers might you want to bring up with the whole class in large-group discussion or lecture? Which issues do you think would be more appropriate for an individual conference? Why?

A Racing Style

Dick Grengs, now in his second year of teaching freshman composition while pursuing a master's degree in medieval studies, has developed a reputation for being an incredibly diligent instructor. He is usually at least a week ahead in his planning, even down to the specifics of his class sessions. He begins working immediately on his students' papers when they turn them in, often staying in his office late into the evening to finish his grading so that he can devote large blocks of time the following day to his own studies. In discussions during his program's TA workshops, he has characterized himself as a "teacher-editor." Students, he feels, are too often coddled in the name of nurturing and would rather have teachers who give them strong, solid, straightforward advice. Once they get over the initial shock of his bluntness, he claims, the students come to appreciate his honesty and learn to accept criticism the way journalists do: as useful, necessary feedback which must not get "all muddled up with ego and self-esteem."

Everything about Dick reflects a highly organized, almost clinically efficient young man impatient to get jobs done well and promptly. He believes that even when students are writing longer academic papers, they should work fast. Mulling over ideas, taking days to "invent" topics and "brainstorm" details, endlessly revising and tinkering with paragraphs and sentences—this is all "the fluff of procrastination." During one meeting, Dick took serious issue with the director's suggestion that four papers over a ten-week term was probably the right number for freshmen. "Four!" Dick blurted out. "I'm doing ten, and even that's probably light. Sure, they're only two or three pages each, but students have to learn to write fast. What's the use giving them two weeks to write one little assignment? When they get out into the real world, they'll be doomed!"

Although Dick has learned much about the "process approach" to teaching writing from his required graduate course for TAs, he rejects many of its principles. Instead of having students work in small groups, he devotes time during many class sessions to solitary writing episodes. Students typically spend fifteen minutes or so writing as quickly and accurately as they can in response to short assignments. These Dick collects and grades. During the rest of each class period, he usually lectures on the principles of good academic writing. He finds that the students seldom complain about his methods because "there are so many chances to do well."

For his second (of ten) short writing assignments, Dick's syllabus reads as follows:

Assignment 2:

Choose something you know well—a sport, hobby, pastime. You're the expert. Write about it so that someone who is not an expert can understand something new about it. Due next Mon. Pls. type!

At the end of the class period before this assignment was due, one of the students somewhat hesitantly approached Dick, who was vigorously erasing the board, and asked if he could "try out" his topic on Dick before beginning the assignment. Continuing to erase the board, Dick asked the student's name.

"Wes—Wes Muelleleile," he replied.

"Look, Wes," Dick said, "my advice is to just blast your way into the paper. Never mind—you'll figure out what you want to say as soon as you sit down to write."

"But I just wanted to see if the kind of writing I want to do is okay for this class," Wes said, "because . . ."

"Don't worry about it, Wes!" Dick interrupted, smiling. "Just do your best, and we'll see how it turns out."

On Monday, Wes turned in the following paper:

Nineties Racing Challenge

In the late 1800's and ealy 1900's bicycle racing was the number one sport in America. Young boys and girls of this era had dreams of growing up and becoming bicycle racers and riding at Madison Square Gardens in New York City in the six day bicycle races.

The racing at this time was brutal and sometimes devastating to these aspiring athletes. Many deaths occured from

riders riding their hearts into oblivian trying to please their
frantic cheering fans.

The public, business world, and press all knew what an
exciting, fast sport cycling was. The bicycle racers of this time
were the highest paid athletes in the world.

Mysteriously by the late 1930's bicycle racing had become
virtually nonexistent with the onset of World War II and the
scarcity of rubber for bike tires. Hundreds of bicycle racing
tracks were destroyed around the country in order to make
room for urban growth.

Recently through enthusiastic American bicycle racers' efforts and Olympic team support people are rediscovering the
benifits cycling has on America. Major United States companies are increasing their advertising coverage of bicycle racing
in order to sell the American public on the outdoor natural
image. Movies are being made to promote the sport of cycling. These efforts are starting to create an interest for cycling again in America.

The United States Cycling Federation is the governing body
for bicycle racing in the United States. The membership of
this organization has risen from 1500 in 1961 to over 50,000
members today. These statistics clearly show that bicycling
racing is on the rise again within the United States.

The new generation of racers are being trianed properly
from early ages. Speed means everything to today's young
racers. These racers are using their resources in turning their
legs into efficient pistons. New training techniques are being
applied and the results have been tremendous. In the past
few years Americans have claimed dozens of world championship medals. But before 1976, Americans had only two
medals in forty years of racing. The results are not coming
from the veteran racers, but from the teenagers of the sport.

The racer of the 1990's has more going for him or her than
any of the predecessors of the old days of bicycle racing. The
United States has some of the world's finest training facilities
for cyclists in the world. New bicycle designs have revolutionized the sport. Instead of the old one-speed balloon tires
clacking across dirt and pebblestone roads, glistening light
alloy bicycles with silk tires are swooshing across our nations
highways.

Todays racers are faced with the challenge of giving back
to the people of America a tradition that is a part of the
history of our country. Modern cyclists are truly luckly to have
the opportunity to be a part of the rebirth of cycling.

After collecting the papers, Dick returned immediately to his office,
made himself a cup of instant coffee, arranged the essays alphabetically,
and set to work. By midafternoon, he had already finished grading
through "Linder" and started in on Wes Muelleleile's paper. Wes's
paper with Dick's comments is shown in Figure 2.

Nineties Racing Challenge

In the late 1800's and ealy 1900's bicycle racing was the number one sport in America. Young boys and girls of this era had dreams of growing up and becoming bicycle racers and riding at Madison Square Gardens in New York City in the six day bicycle races.

The racing at this time was brutal and sometimes devastating to these aspiring athletes. Many deaths occured from riders riding their hearts into oblivian trying to please their frantic cheering fans.

The public, business world, and press all knew what an exciting, fast sport cycling was. The bicycle racers of this time were the highest paid athletes in the world.

Mysteriously by the late 1930's bicycle racing had become virtually nonexistent with the onset of World War II and the scarcity of rubber for bike tires. Hundreds of bicycle racing tracks were destroyed around the country in order to make room for urban growth.

Recently through enthusiastic American bicycle racers' efforts and Olympic team support people are rediscovering the benifits cycling has on America. Major United States companies are increasing their advertising coverage of bicycle racing in order to sell the American public on the outdoor natural image. Movies are being made to promote the sport of cycling. These efforts are starting to create an interest for cycling again in America.

The United States Cycling Federation is the governing body for bicycle racing in the United States. The membership of this organization has risen from 1500 in 1961 to over 50,000 members today. These statistics clearly show that bicycling racing is on the rise again within the United States.

The new generation of racers are being trained properly from early ages. Speed means everything to today's young racers. These racers are using their resources in turning their legs into efficient pistons. New training techniques are being applied and the results have been tremendous.

In the past few years Americans have claimed dozens of world championship medals. But before 1976, Americans had only two medals in forty years of racing. The results are not coming from the veteran racers, but from the teenagers of the sport.

The racer of the 1990's has more going for him or her than any of the predecessors of the old days of bicycle racing. The United States has some of the world's finest training facilities for cyclists in the world. New bicycle designs have revolutionized the sport. Instead of the old one-speed balloon tires clacking across dirt and pebblestone roads, glistening light alloy bicycles with silk tires are swooshing across our nations highways.

Todays racers are faced with the challenge of giving back to the people of America a tradition that is a part of the history of our country. Modern cyclists are truly luckly to have the opportunity to be a part of the rebirth of cycling.

Handwritten marginal comments: No ¶ break; No ¶ break; passive; This should be an adverb, not an adjective; weak and clumsy phrasing; with these reasons, what is so mysterious about the nonexistence of racing?; trite; wordy; How does this sentence follow the one before or lead into the one after?; awk.; word choice; wordy; what is the logic of your argument?; redundant; wordy; Cliche'; wordy; Tense; phrases such as these are cop-outs from using real details. It makes the reader lose all confidence in what you say.; This ¶ is wordy & choppy & could be written in one sentence. In fact, this information should have been the topic sentence for the following ¶.; redundant; wordy; "of our country" or "of our sports"?

Handwritten summary comment: Your topic is excellent, and your focus is well under control, but 2 problems turn up so often that, as a reader, I was disturbed and even angered. Firstly, you seem to have no sense of ¶ structure nor where to divide ¶s. Secondly, your writing is full of clutter. You have too many poorly worded phrases and sentences, too many unnecessary words & phrases, too much confusion. Why do you allow your writing to be so difficult? Your topic is so good, but you undercut it with your sloppy presentation. Both of your problems — unorganized ¶s and disorganized speech — compromise your ideas to low levels. (D)

Figure 2. Dick's comments and corrections on Wes's paper.

At the end of the next class period, after Dick had turned back the graded papers, Wes once again came up as Dick was erasing the board.

"Excuse me, Mr. Grengs, but I was wondering if you could take another look at my paper on bike racing."

"Why?" Dick said over his shoulder, continuing to erase the board.

"Well," Wes went on hesitantly, "I really don't think I deserve a *D*."

"It's Wes, right?" Dick said, turning toward him. "See, I have a policy of not reconsidering my grades, Wes. Your paper's done, and it's time to move on. Let's devote our energy to the next assignment and put this one away in a drawer somewhere."

Wes had rolled his paper up into a tube and was turning it around and around in his hands. "But I think you didn't understand my paragraphs," he said. "I was trying to make them short and fast, sort of like racing and also sort of like the sports magazines I read. I mean, stuff in *Bicycle World* just doesn't have these long, drawn-out, thesis-type paragraphs and topic sentences and all that. Do you see what I was trying to do?"

ISSUES FOR DISCUSSION

• Reflect on Dick's comments on Wes's paper. How do they compare with the comments you would have made?

• Dick's comments reflect his teaching philosophy. How would you describe that philosophy? Does that philosophy justify Dick's priorities in commenting? Why or why not?

• Wes is troubled by Dick's comments (and grade) in part because he does not feel Dick has understood his *intentions* in his essay. How much does judgment about "surface" matters of style, paragraph length, wording, and so forth need to depend on a writer's intentions?

• If Dick had asked the students to write a purpose statement explaining who they had in mind as their audience, why they were writing, and why they had made certain choices of style, structure, and the like, do you think he would have graded Wes's paper any differently? Why or why not?

• What issues in Wes's paper might you want to bring up with the whole class in large-group discussion or lecture? Which issues do you think would be more appropriate for an individual conference? Why?

Lapses in Aptness

In this scenario, we would like you to respond to a student paper written for a developmental writing class. The paper was written in response to an assignment asking the students how they would schedule their time so that they would succeed in college.

The paper below was submitted by Carla Kambic as a final draft of the assignment. Read and respond to this paper as if Carla were a member of your class.

Make your comments on the paper before you proceed to the next part of the scenario.

Scheduling My Time

My estimate of my time resulted in all the opposite with reality. The first week, I estimated what I planned to study at a specific time everyday. The first couple of days I went strictly by the schedule I had made. Suddenly, I started getting interupted every hour, either the telephone rang or my brother would bother me. So eventually I was finishing my homework late and the first schedule was totally useless.

The second week I made another schedule in which I added some time to talk on the phone. This method did not work because I would receive calls even when I was scheduled to do my homework. This new schedule did not work either so I tried the third week without planning a schedule and just did my homework whenever I could. I also realized during the third week I was studying some of my subjects more than others because I didn't have a schedule to follow.

I finally realized I needed definitely a schedule to go by, but with fewer interruptions such as the phone calls, my boyfriend, and my brother. I was determined to give up some of my time with them in order to go by an effective schedule. I told my friends I had to do my homework and if they could please call at a certain time, the time I had scheduled for breaks, they didn't mind. On the other hand, my boyfriend was upset with my decision to spend less time with him, but we try to see each other over the weekends and that's better than not seeing each other at all.

This exercise proved to be very useful because it made me realize I carelessly spent my time and I didn't spend equal time on each subject as I should have. By scheduling my time and following it, I still have time to enjoy myself and study effectively and that to me was the purpose of this assignment.

Terry Feldman, Carla's teacher, is a conscientious writing instructor who believes that the craft of writing is just that—the process of carefully crafting sentences built of balanced, fluent clauses that elegantly move the logic of the discourse forward. Terry is resigned to spending long hours correcting—by rewriting—the flawed sentences in his students' papers. But he is convinced that the time is well spent. He believes that the students will be able to correct their own errors later in the course.

Sentence-level revisions are time consuming for teachers and troublesome for students. More often than not, when Terry reads student papers with pronoun reference problems, punctuation, or unwieldy or awkward sentence constructions, he spends time puzzling out possible solutions to those specific problems so that the students will be able to revise their own worst sentences in the next assignment. He is convinced that this hard work will pay off in the students' learning and show him to be a helpful, diligent writing instructor.

Carla's paper with Terry's comments and corrections is shown in Figure 3.

ISSUES FOR DISCUSSION

• How do your comments on Carla's paper compare with Terry's? How long do you think it took Terry to respond in this way?

• What do you think Carla will learn from Terry's method of responding?

• Construct a taxonomy of types of corrections, additions, deletions, and comments that Terry makes on this paper. What observations can you make about the array of issues and corrections addressed?

• Here is Terry's final comment written at the bottom of Carla's paper:

> Carla: I've noticed that both your sentences and papers as a
> whole are becoming shorter and simpler. Try to experiment
> with more complex sentence structure in future papers.

Terry has made an important observation about Carla's development as a writer. Why do you think this is happening in Carla's work?

• Some teachers assign split grades to papers, giving one grade for mechanics, grammar, and usage, and another for content. How do you feel about that option? Would split grading help or hinder Terry in accomplishing his purposes?

• Terry uses the word "correcting" to describe what he does with students' papers. Terms used by other teachers include "responding to," "grading," "evaluating," "commenting on," "marking," "editing," "providing feedback," and "facilitating revision." Which of these or other terms would you use to describe what you did when you reviewed Carla's paper?

• What issues in Carla's paper might you want to bring up with the whole class in large-group discussion or lecture? What issues do you think would be more appropriate for an individual conference? Why?

[handwritten top right: This means to reverse the order]

Carla Kambic
Composition
Mr. Feldman

SCHEDULING MY TIME

[handwritten: how's spend] *[handwritten: Contrasted sharply]*

My estimate of ~~my time resulted in all the opposite~~ with reality. The first week, I estimated what I planned to study at a specific time everyday. The first couple of days I went strictly by the schedule. ~~I had made. Suddenly, I started getting~~ *[handwritten: Unfortunately / was]* *[handwritten right margin: word choice / logic]* interrupted every hour; either the telephone rang or my brother would bother me. So eventually I was finishing my homework late and the first schedule was totally useless.

[handwritten left margin: The meaning of suddenly does not go with every hour]

The second week I made another schedule ~~in~~ which I *[to]* added some time to talk on the phone. This method did not work because I ~~would~~ received calls even when I was scheduled to do my homework. ~~This~~ new schedule did not *[Since / began]* work ~~either, so~~ I ~~tried~~ the third week without ~~planning~~ a schedule; ~~and~~ just did my homework whenever I could. I ~~also~~ realized during the third week I was studying some of my subjects ~~more than others~~ because I didn't have a schedule to follow. *[I / for less time than I should have]*

I finally ~~realized~~ I needed definitely a schedule *[admitted that]* ~~to go by,~~ but with fewer interruptions ~~such as~~ the *[planned / for]* phone calls, my boyfriend, and my brother. I was *[and visits with]* determined to give up some of my time with them in order to ~~go by an effective~~ schedule. I told my *[adhere to a strict]* friends I had to do my homework, and ~~if they could~~ *[that / asked them to]* please call at a certain time; the time I had scheduled *[s/]* for breaks, they didn't mind. ~~On the other hand,~~ my *[and]* boyfriend was upset with my decision to spend less time *[initially]* with him, but we try to see each other over the *[now]* weekends and that's better than not seeing each other at all.

This exercise proved to be very useful because it *[that]* made me realize I ~~carelessly~~ spent my time, and I didn't *[Carelessly / that]* spend ~~equal~~ time on each subject. ~~as I should have.~~ By *[An appropriate amount of]* scheduling my time and following ~~it,~~ I still have time *[the schedule]* to enjoy myself and study effectively, and that to me was the purpose of this assignment.

[handwritten left margin: logic]
[handwritten right margin: it - antecedent is Time]

[handwritten: logic — you probably don't need to spend the same amount of time on each subject.]

[handwritten note at bottom:]
Carla,
Get to the writing clinic right away! Bring this with you if you like. Ask your tutor to make a list of things you need to work on and begin a systematic program to improve ~~your style~~ the aptness of your expression.
T. F.

Figure 3. Terry's comments and corrections on Carla's paper.

5 Managing Discourse in Classes, Conferences, and Small Groups

Some colleges and universities have a surprising course requirement for students who are preparing to become teachers: they must take a beginning course in acting and directing. But the need for good teachers to be effective actors and directors should not be surprising. A substantial part of the art of teaching consists of knowing both how to present yourself to the "audience" of your class and how to "direct" the activities of your "cast of characters," the students. This is not to say that the teacher must be overly theatrical or the class merely an occasion for performance. It is just that effective teachers are people who have learned to present themselves well and to stage their classroom activities.

Faculty members in all fields must learn to play several roles, but the need to strike a balance between teacher presentation—commonly called lecturing—and student interaction—both traditional discussion and innovative forms of collaborative learning—is especially important in writing classes. There is an adage that no one ever learned much about how to write by listening to someone talk about writing, so instructors must fight the temptation to stand in front of the class and lecture too much. The prevailing wisdom in writing instruction for years has been that students learn most effectively by *doing*—by writing frequently, sharing their work with others, getting and giving feedback, and revising. But even these process-oriented activities have their dangers: some students, either by nature or by convention, are hesitant about interacting with others in class, and instructors need to learn how to guide these students into the participatory stream.

The nature of this interaction has, in recent years, become even more important with the increasing use of collaborative learning and small-group work in the writing class. Working with students in groups entails benefits and drawbacks. The principal benefit is that students working collaboratively have the opportunity to become active learners, to teach each other, and thus to learn more effectively. The major drawback is that, in a group, not every student is going to share the workload equally, and often questions may arise concerning who ought to be given credit for what work.

As is the case with managing small groups, learning how to interact with students in private conferences requires some savvy. First, instructors need to remember that most students in writing courses, especially beginning college courses, have *never* had a student-teacher conference before unless they were in some kind of trouble. Because high school teachers' workloads are so heavy and their time so booked up, most of them simply do not have the chance to work with students individually or in groups. In addition, instructors need to realize that meeting with students in conference alters the interpersonal dynamics that the classroom establishes. In other words, students often see a different person sitting at a desk in an office than the person they see in front of the classroom.

The scenarios in this chapter offer new teachers the opportunity to discuss issues of managing one's roles as an instructor: how to guide the class, how to set up and manage small groups, and how to interact with students in private conferences. Although not exhaustive in their coverage of these issues, the scenarios should prompt discussion beyond the boundaries of their content, to the larger issues of professional role, character, and direction in writing courses.

Master Thespian

Keith Delattre is a second-year teaching assistant assigned for the first time to teach the introduction to business writing. Keith's first year of teaching was marked by general success—his students liked him, he felt very much engaged in their learning, and his evaluations were, for the most part, above average. Several minor problems came up during the year, including a discrepancy in his grading criteria and a complaint from a student who did not understand Keith's (unwritten) policies on turning in rough drafts; but these he handled fairly and diplomatically.

Keith's teaching style follows a general pattern: typically, he begins his classes with a short (fifteen-minute) presentation, which he calls a "minilecture," and then he asks the students to apply the principles or concepts from the presentation to their own or each other's writing, usually in small groups or individually. After moving about the room during the activity, he reconvenes the whole class for ten or fifteen minutes of discussion. For Keith, this pattern not only helps him organize his class, but also provides a model of learning which he hopes his students can use in other contexts. He even has names for each stage: "Introducing" is the stage at which new ideas, perspectives, or theories are presented in their raw form. The second stage, "Applying," helps the students to integrate new ideas into the old through direct application to their own work. The final stage, "Reinforcing," helps him to strengthen the students' tentative links between theory and application by recapitulating the new ideas in the context of what the students did (and what he observed them doing) in the application stage.

Keith also believes that his minilectures must be as animated as possible because "even fifteen minutes of one-way, teacher-to-student talk is usually enough to lull most students into semiconsciousness." For this reason, observers of Keith's classes characterize him as "almost theatrical" in his demeanor. He moves quickly about the room in an animated way, varies the pitch and loudness of his voice, peppers his talk with jokes and asides, and often uses an overhead projector, which allows him to gesticulate toward the screen or move between it and the blackboard to "keep the students' eyes open." Whenever he can, he wants to turn his minilectures into "something like a blend of educational TV, standup comedy, and charismatic preaching." Several students have pointed out in his course evaluations that this style takes some getting used to.

Keith has been teaching his business writing class for less than two weeks. The students have seemed energetic and interested. It is about midway into the first short paper, in which the students must draft a letter applying for a job they would love to have. To do so, they must research positions in their field of interest by locating newspaper ads and analyzing the stated criteria.

It is Wednesday, and Keith has spent more than an hour planning his class session. The students are bringing rough drafts of their job application letters, and he has decided to focus his minilecture on the principles of revision: what he means by *revision*, why he thinks it is essential in all writing, and what sorts of specific questions students should ask about each other's papers in order to improve them.

Keith feels very strongly about his theory of revision: students should learn to throw out first attempts, cross out whole sections of prose, and look upon their early work as messy and tentative. He feels that most students do not understand revision and think that a decent first attempt is all they *should* attempt. He also believes that students need to rethink the idea of "owning" a text, especially their early drafts. If other ideas, people, and so forth influence the progression of the draft, he reasons, no one yet has a rightful claim to its words or ideas. Drafts are, in other words, communal property, and anyone can "write on and into them."

Toward the end of his minilecture, Keith is feeling especially confident. The students seem to be in generally high spirits, laughing at his jokes, attending studiously to his points and his carefully prepared overhead illustrating the main principles of revision in business writing.

At the end of his presentation (and after one last joke that meets with a burst of laughter from the class), Keith pauses and asks if there are any questions before the students form small groups to read and respond to each other's drafts. Pam, a young woman who usually does not volunteer to talk, hesitantly raises her hand. What should someone do, she asks, if their draft doesn't need any revision? Privately horrified that the student has not attended to a word he has said, Keith asks what could possibly have possessed Pam to think that her first attempt, no matter how initially effective, would not need any further revision. Nervously, Pam explains that her draft is actually a letter she wrote several months before for a part-time job at a large local law firm. She knows the letter was effective because she was instantly granted an interview and then hired for the position.

Keith, who has now moved over toward Pam, asks for her letter. Backing up to the middle of the room, he holds the letter in front of him with outstretched arms. Feeling the tension in Keith's demeanor, the class seems to be holding its breath in anticipation.

"Do you know what we do with drafts like this?" Keith asks, a devilish smile on his face. The class is riveted to him. Pam sits, motionless, her eyes fixed on the carefully typed draft now dangling at the very ends of Keith's fingertips. "We do like this!" And, with one clean motion, Keith tears the page into two almost identical pieces. There is an audible gasp from the class. He moves precisely over to Pam, as if measuring each motion, and lays the torn pieces neatly in the center of her desk. "Any questions?" he asks.

Within a few seconds, Pam has turned bright red. Her eyes brimming with tears, she quickly gathers her papers and notebooks and dashes from the room. The class listens, paralyzed, as her sobs echo down the hall of the building. Without mentioning the incident, Keith proceeds to form the students into small groups.

The next day, Keith receives a note from the director of his composition program. Apparently, Pam has asked to be transferred to another section, but the program usually frowns on this practice because most of the other sections are full and a switch would require over-enrolling someone else's course. The note ends with a request to set up an appointment to discuss the matter.

ISSUES FOR DISCUSSION

• Given Keith's beliefs about revision and text ownership, was his action justified? Why or why not?

- What should Keith tell the director when he meets with her? How should he explain the incident?
- What should Keith do about Pam? Should he set up a conference with her? What should he tell her in this conference? Should he persuade her to stay in his class? Why or why not?
- Should Keith privately apologize to Pam? Should he publicly apologize to her in his classroom? Should he say anything about the incident to the class, and if so, what? Is he at "fault"?
- Keith's theatrical teaching style lent itself to his tearing up Pam's paper. Should he change this style? Why or why not? How much should teachers avoid making spontaneous remarks or acting on the spur of the moment in a teaching situation? Should Keith slow his pace?

"Chill Out, Gringo Fool!"

In teaching her writing class, Jane Baker often used outside articles, essays, and editorials as well as student texts to raise questions that students might answer in an essay and to show how others frame their arguments for certain readers. She was particularly interested in strategies that persuade; she wanted students to realize that listing facts, employing a logical progression, and establishing authority are not the only tools of argumentation.

During the first class of a week early in the term, she had discussed several logical fallacies: ad hominem, begging the question, circular reasoning, false analogy, non sequitur, post hoc, red herring, and slippery slope. Students constructed their own examples of each type of fallacy, wrote them on the board, and discussed them. Then she turned to the uses of humor and wordplay in persuasion.

In preparation for this part of the class, Jane told the students to read Barbara Ehrenreich's "Farewell to Work," an article on the debate about the English Only amendment. This was a timely topic because some states were considering amendments that would restrict stores from operating in Spanish. As a prereading activity, Jane asked the class to consider how Ehrenreich's audience might differ from the audience of a regular newspaper story or scholarly article. She wrote their ideas on the board. She also asked them to consider what strategies Ehrenreich might use to address this audience. The students suggested that humor as well as facts would attract the audience they imagined.

In light of these predictions, the class was to read the article carefully, responding to the humor and marking Ehrenreich's construction of her arguments and her use of the strategies discussed previously. Jane did not say so, but she hoped the students would note the humor in Ehrenreich's use of a mock narrator like the one in Swift's *A Modest Proposal*. She particularly hoped they would note the wordplay and humor in the hyperbolic arguments that the word *quiche* should become *egg pie,* that bilingualism has made Canada "large, cold, and boring," and that all our national woes began with the importation of words like "existentialism, fascism, and french fries."

When the students came to class the next day, Jane could feel the excitement in the atmosphere. She assumed they were enthusiastic about discussing the arguments in the article. But what happened was that the usually thoughtful class degenerated into a series of personal invectives against people who speak Spanish. Some students complained about having trouble understanding those they had encountered in their personal experiences: shopkeepers, clerks, attendants. Comments were generally along the lines of, "Once I was in a store and I couldn't buy a blouse because the sales ladies were all speaking Spanish." Others in the class agreed and wanted a chance to list their grievances. Although Jane generally welcomed personal responses, she was disturbed by their stereotyping, prejudice, and sweeping generalizations. She tried to bring the class back to a discussion of Ehrenreich's arguments—her reasons for urging cultural diversity, her point that English is already composed of other languages, her humorous argument that hostility toward non-English speakers often represents a misguided paranoia (for example, that *no fumar* means "chill out, gringo fool"), and her extreme future scenarios of a strictly "English" language.

One student, Sam Jorgensen, the most talkative member of the class, persisted in arguing against any of Ehrenreich's claims that Jane attempted to point out. Her exasperation must have shown, because he blurted out, "Why are you looking at me that way? Don't you want to hear our opinion?"

ISSUES FOR DISCUSSION

• How should Jane respond to Sam's outburst and to the cultural biases of the class?

• How explicit should Jane's own opinion be in the classroom?

• Should Jane allow a discussion to continue when she perceives the students' opinions to be "wrong," or at least ill-informed?

• In general, should conflicts that occur in class discussion be addressed directly or in private conference?

• Jane chose this article to highlight specific argumentative strategies.

Is it realistic for her to expect students to suspend their feelings about the topic of an article while analyzing the ways in which the topic is presented?

"I Prefer Not To"

When Rhea Sorkon took a graduate-level seminar on teaching English to prepare to teach her own sections of the university's introductory writing course the following term, she learned how to use a popular technique called "author's chair." The technique is very simple: one day each week, a student brings to class enough copies of a rough draft he or she is working on to distribute to every member of the class. Then the student stands in front of the class and reads the paper aloud while the others follow along. As they are reading, class members put a straight line beside any portion of the draft they feel is specifically praiseworthy, and they put a wavy line beside any passage they think needs reworking. Finally, each student writes a comment on the bottom of the paper, and the reader gets all of the other students' marked and commented-upon papers back to consult during revision.

When Rhea first saw this technique being demonstrated, it worked beautifully. The author for the day read her draft clearly, slowly, and loudly. The instructor whose class Rhea was observing had obviously used the technique before and had taught her students how to offer concrete, specific responses that would really help the author revise her draft. Rhea listened attentively as the class members praised the author's clear, distinctive thesis but pointed out one idea that most believed ought to appear earlier in the essay and one passage where she needed to provide more examples. They also commented on the author's successful use of an occasional short sentence for emphasis but noted her tendency to overuse the sentence fragment so that a couple of passages seemed almost telegraphic in style. And they noted the author's intelligent linking of related clauses with conjunctive adverbs like *however* and *therefore* but pointed out that using such words to join clauses requires a semicolon.

Aha, Rhea thought, here finally is writing as a social activity. Student writers are trying out their drafts with an audience of their peers. The students are responding adult to adult. They are not picking at each other's work; they are not merely pointing out mistakes; they are collaborating. This writing is *real*, Rhea thought. And she was determined that when she taught her own section of this course next term, author's chair sessions would play a central role in her pedagogy.

Rhea's class got off to a rousing start the following term. She had a full complement of twenty students, so she planned to have two students conduct author's chair sessions every Friday, beginning with the third week. That would give everyone a chance to have his or her paper critiqued at least once by the end of the term. On Friday of the second week, Rhea brought in a draft of an essay she was writing for a course so that she could sit in the author's chair. She wanted to do this for two reasons: first, to show her students that she, too, was a writer learning her craft and, second, to model for them the kinds of responses she wanted to get from the students during these sessions. She did not want the students to become just picky error monitors. She wanted substantive, helpful responses. It worked exactly as she planned. The students were amazed to see that their teacher was a practicing writer herself. They learned during the session how to respond to a paper first holistically and then analytically, considering in order a paper's quality, organization, and development of ideas; sentence style and diction; and spelling, punctuation, and usage. So far, so good, Rhea thought.

On the following Friday, the students began taking the author's chair. Rhea had determined to proceed alphabetically through the roster, so Ruby Alvarado and Marcus Brown were up. Although both students were a little embarrassed to go first, they performed bravely. Both read their papers a little too fast and indistinctly, but Rhea succeeded in slowing them down and improving their diction. In response to Ruby's paper, many students still wanted only to correct her punctuation and point out words she had misspelled, so Rhea had to work hard to elicit commentary on issues of a higher level as well. The students caught on to the idea of holistic and analytic response again, and their comments about Marcus's draft were much fuller and more directed toward helping him revise his paper at all levels—ideas, style, and "grammar."

The two students scheduled to "get the chair," as the students playfully put it, the next Friday were Binh Cho and Pamela Curtis. This was the fourth week, and Rhea was getting to know most of the students, but Binh was a mystery to her. He never said a word in class. She learned from the course roster that he was a junior majoring in engineering. There was one other upper-division student in the class, but the other eighteen were freshmen. The essay he produced for the in-class, diagnostic writing sample during the first week was short and full of first-language interference problems: the use of articles was erratic and incorrect, the verb forms were often wrong, and many of the sentences were fragmented. Rhea had noted these problems and, without filling his diagnostic with red-ink corrections, had urged Binh to be sure to go to the university's writing center for help on his essays. His first paper, which he turned in on time at the beginning of the third week, was not quite so riddled with first-language interference problems. Clearly, she thought, Binh can do better if he has time to revise and if he gets help.

When Rhea arrived in class, she found twenty copies of Binh's draft sitting on her desk. She conducted a little class business—reminding students about their assignment, asking to see a couple of students during her office hours—then asked Binh to come to the front of the room, read his draft aloud, and get into the chair. Binh did not move. He did not even look at her. He sat slumped in his chair, staring straight forward. Rhea began to pass the copies of Binh's paper around and asked him again to come to the front of the room to read. Still no response. The tension in the room was palpable. "Okay," Rhea announced, "let's have Pamela go first today."

This seemed to break the tension. Pamela Curtis came forward, handing a stack of her papers to a fellow student to start distributing as she left her seat. She read her paper, and the class spent a productive twenty minutes offering her specific praise and suggestions for revision at the idea, style, and mechanics and usage levels.

Then it was Binh's turn again. "There's no more delaying, Binh," Rhea said, trying not to sound annoyed. Binh did not flinch, and the tension was back in the air. "Very well," Rhea said, her voice rising, "I'll read your paper aloud for you." Rhea took a look at the first paragraph and saw that all the first-language interference mistakes from the diagnostic essay were back in this draft. In the first paragraph alone, there were articles misused and missing, incorrect verb forms, egregious sentence fragments. Without pausing, Rhea began to read Binh's paper loudly, slowly, and distinctly, exactly as it was written. The missing and wrong articles were completely evident; the incorrect verb forms and the sentence fragments sounded totally ludicrous. Rhea paused at the end of the first paragraph, wondering whether she should continue. She looked up and made eye contact, first with the class as a whole and then with Binh. During this brief pause, a few students in the back of the room began to giggle quietly.

Binh shot up out of his seat and strode from the room, slamming the door on the way out.

ISSUES FOR DISCUSSION

• What should Rhea do the very minute after Binh has slammed the door to the classroom?

- What should Rhea do, if anything, to try to make contact with Binh after this session?

- Should Rhea stop using author's chair in this class? in future classes? Why or why not?

- Assuming that Rhea continues using author's chair, how can she avoid such unpleasant situations?

Slices of Professional Life

What follows are some "slices of life" taken from the experiences of several first-year teachers of college writing courses. Each of these brief scenarios raises questions about managing classroom discourse.

What's in a Name

Frieda Stolz is a twenty-four-year-old beginning doctoral student in English and a teaching assistant. As a TA, she teaches two sections of the introductory writing course at her university. Near the end of the first class session in the semester, one of the students raises his hand and asks politely, "Excuse me, uh . . . I have a question, but I don't know what to call you?"

ISSUES FOR DISCUSSION

- How should Frieda respond to the student's concern?
- Does it matter how students, especially in a writing class, refer to their teachers in direct address? Why or why not?

Young at Heart

Steve Moriarty, a twenty-three-year-old graduate student and teaching assistant, also teaches introductory writing courses regularly. He is one of those people who will look young forever. Moreover, as a student himself, he frequently dresses very casually: in warm weather, shorts, a tee shirt of some sort, and tennis shoes or sandals. One day near the end of the first week of a semester, Steve had just begun teaching a class session. At five minutes past the hour, he was distributing a handout and beginning to explain it, when a young man who had not yet attended the class came strolling into the room. In a loud voice, this new arrival crowed, "This Comp. 101, section 88456? Yo, looks like loads of fun, don't it?" Steve replied quickly, "Excuse me! Yes, this is Comp. 101, 88456, and we're trying to get class started. Please

have a seat, if you're in this class, and see me personally at the end."
The stranger looked Steve over carefully. "Well, *excuse me,* Mr. Teacher,"
he said, doing a pretty rotten Eddie Haskell imitation. "I have mistooken
you for one of the pupils in this enterprise!"

ISSUES FOR DISCUSSION

• How should Steve respond to this student?

• Since Steve is and looks so young—like a contemporary of his
students—should he do anything about his appearance or behavior to
establish himself as the instructor?

Pre-Prof

Gwen Sweeney is in her first year of graduate school and her first year
of a teaching assistantship in the department of English. During the
first term, she taught an introductory writing course. During the second
semester, she is leading a discussion section for an introduction to
literature class, and she enjoys a good bit of freedom in what goes on
in the meetings of the discussion section. The first week, she had her
students read Robert Frost's poem "Mending Walls" and required them
to write a short essay explicating the theme, "Good fences make good
neighbors." She intended to use these essays as her opportunity to get
an initial assessment of the students' writing abilities.

In her commentary on the essays, Gwen focused only on the students'
organizational abilities, style, spelling, usage, and mechanics, and not
on their main ideas, their notions of what "Good fences make good
neighbors" means. Nonetheless, as she was returning the papers in both
classes, she felt compelled to comment on two or three really aberrant
readings of this line: "Well, I'm only a TA, but that isn't what that line
means to me."

ISSUES FOR DISCUSSION

• Is there anything wrong with Gwen's prefacing her comment about
the papers in this way?

• If you are a teaching assistant, what should you say to your students—
explicitly and implicitly through your behavior—about your title, your
duties, your responsibilities, your "power," and so on?

A Student Trashes an Office Mate

As a first-year instructor, Michael Barrientos shares his office with two
others, Luther Bridgeman and Angela Hills. The arrangement is not

too inconvenient because the three instructors' schedules are different enough that each is almost always alone there for student conferences. Their students, however, sometimes have a tough time remembering their instructor's office hours, and often a student will come searching for one of the other two when Michael is in the office. He has gotten to know a handful of Luther's and Angela's students from these passing encounters.

One of Angela's students, Bobby Pryzinski, presented a problem for Michael. The first time Bobby came looking for Angela, he struck up a conversation with Michael. During this talk, Bobby learned that Michael and Angela were teaching different sections of the same introductory composition course. About a week later, Bobby showed up again, ostensibly looking for Angela, and was carrying a copy of a paper she had recently returned. Bobby looked terribly upset, and Michael asked him what was troubling him. Bobby blurted out, "She just gave us back our papers, and the bitch gave me a *D*. She doesn't know what she's talking about. I bet you wouldn't give me a *D* on this paper. Would you read it and tell me what you think of it?"

ISSUE FOR DISCUSSION

• What would you do if you were Michael in this situation? Explain your course of action.

Virginia Teaches Barthes

Virginia Oldham discovered contemporary literary theory in her second year as a doctoral student in English. During one semester, she read major works by Roland Barthes, Michel Foucault, Jacques Derrida, and Luce Irigaray, applying their concepts to both "canonical" and "marginalized" literary works. It was an exhilarating experience for her: no longer did she see literature as comprising a body of standard works, whose themes, motifs, and techniques she would have to learn by heart. Literature was now a dancing of signifiers, a dialectic of aporias and closures, a working out of deep psychosocial complexes. She was thrilled with the vigor of her graduate work. All the while, she was teaching her requisite two sections of general, introductory college composition. Early in the term, she decided to give a lecture on the phallologocentrism of the five-paragraph theme. When a student asked her to clarify the theme of a short story they were reading in class, Virginia cried out in despair, "Oh, you can't mean you want closure, can you?"

ISSUE FOR DISCUSSION

• What do you think is the ideal relation between what graduate students learn in their courses and the principles, methods, and materials they use to teach their introductory classes?

Coco Feels Raped

Several days after the end of his introductory writing class, Terry Macewicz was in his office, tidying up from a hectic semester, when Coco Stebbings walked into the room. The students in his class, both men and women, thought Coco was absolutely gorgeous, and Terry had had trouble on several occasions keeping the male students focused on the classwork when he put them with her into small groups. He knew that some men in the class were constantly talking about Coco and were riveted to her when she spoke out in discussions. The women, for their part, seemed preoccupied with Coco's expensive clothes and chic hairstyle. All the attention to Coco's appearance was, Terry felt, unfortunate because she had a keenly analytical mind and an articulate way of speaking, but the other students seemed to pay much more attention to her good looks than to her ideas. Now she was in his office visibly upset.

"Hi, Coco," Terry said. "Congratulations on the *A*."

"Look, Mr. Macewicz," Coco replied firmly, "I haven't come to complain about my grade or anything about your teaching, and I did get a lot out of the class. But I feel that you have absolutely no sense of protecting people's privacy in your courses. First you suggested that we exchange phone numbers with members of our conference group so we can get together outside of class. Well, you should know that ever since the first week of class I've been getting nuisance calls in my dorm room and both my roommate and I are terrified. Then I started getting lewd notes under my door, and when I got together with Tom Bonaventure to work on our group project, all he did was try making a pass at me and I had to finish it by myself. Then you read my paper about my ski trip with my boyfriend out loud to the class and I got all sorts of remarks from several guys in the class every time they saw me. Then you left our papers in a box in the hall outside your office where everyone can get at them, and someone has stolen my final project. And to top it all off you pinned your grade sheet up on your door where everyone can see my address and social security number and my grade. I feel like everything you've done in this class has just stripped me naked. I feel like I've been raped."

ISSUES FOR DISCUSSION

• How should Terry respond to Coco's accusations?

• Which of Terry's actions do you find unacceptable in the context of Coco's rights to privacy? How would you describe those rights: psychologically? politically? as a matter of personal safety?

• Are any of Terry's actions defensible and, if so, on what grounds?

• What are Terry's legal responsibilities to maintain his students' right to privacy? Do you know of specific institutional policies where you teach that bear on Terry's actions and related activities in and out of the classroom?

Swearing Up and Down

Jim Sites collected his first set of papers the second week of the semester. He knew that his responses to these first papers would set the tone for the whole term, and he had conscientiously set aside most of the weekend to read them leisurely. He was feeling surprisingly confident as he moved through the first six or seven essays, but then he read a paper that hit him like a punch to the solar plexus. One student, who had never given him much cause for concern during class, had unleashed a vicious stream of obscenities on the page. The invective was not aimed directly at Jim, but rather at life's unfairness in general, his ex-girlfriend's unfaithfulness, and the stupidity of the assignment. Jim sat, stunned, staring at the paper.

ISSUES FOR DISCUSSION

• What would you do in this situation? How would you respond to the student?

• Should Jim consult a mentor or supervisor? Why or why not?

Coming Out

Norma Prather is an energetic, take-charge sort of person. For two years before entering the graduate English program, she worked as an editor for a trade publication. During those years, her social life had been completely separate from her professional life. She was looking forward to combining the relaxed social environment of the graduate community with the rigorous intellectual challenge of her graduate career.

Early into the semester, Norma sought out the gay and lesbian graduate group on campus and made time to participate in the group's activities. She was quite open about her sexual orientation among the graduate students in her department, but she wondered if she should share this information with her freshman writing classes. One of her gay colleagues who had done so said it had made his teaching more difficult, but another had argued that the students actually appreciated his honesty and had thought more deeply about the issue of sexual orientation in connection with some of their position papers.

ISSUE FOR DISCUSSION

• If Norma consulted you for advice, what would you suggest about this issue?

Psyched by Style

In place of a standard handbook in his freshman composition course, Tony Dexter decided to use Richard Lanham's book on style because he liked its brief but memorable devices for helping students improve their sentence structure. One day he asked his students to work on a sentence-rewriting exercise in the book. In this exercise, Lanham showed how he rewrote a sentence that he had found in a psychology paper. The original sentence had several nominalizations and a passive verb; Lanham rewrote it to eliminate the nominalizations and recast the verb to active. Several of Tony's students protested, arguing that if they were to write like Lanham in a psychology course they would not get *A*'s but *C*'s.

ISSUES FOR DISCUSSION

• How should Tony respond?

• To what extent should a writing instructor critique the concepts of good writing or the grading policies of another discipline?

Collaboration or Collusion?

Peggy McIngalls was teaching freshman composition at a large university for the first time. Her approach, common in her department, was a mixture of writing-as-process and writing based on the critical analysis of various readings on social and political issues.

At the start of the course, Peggy spent some time explaining how students should cite material from the readings in their papers. She devoted two class sessions to the various ways that a writer can incorporate someone else's words and ideas into a piece of original writing (summary, paraphrase, quotation), as well as the procedures for citing this other work (footnotes, endnotes, in-text references, and so forth). The students practiced these strategies, using sample texts until Peggy was satisfied that they not only understood the importance of documentation, but also could manage the citation process with reasonable facility.

For the second paper in the course (a "problem-solution report"), Peggy formed the students into working groups of three or four. Each group was to choose an issue from the course readings, search for additional material on the topic in the library, and then create a single, collaboratively written paper synthesizing the views on the issue and making recommendations for its possible resolution. Peggy knew she was taking a certain risk, never before having navigated her way through the complexities of assigning group grades and assessing individuals' performance in the group. She reasoned that her emphasis on gathering, critiquing, and documenting outside texts would be reinforced by the need for students to accommodate each other's ideas and weave their separate voices into a single, seamless paper. Final papers were to include a "process overview," which would summarize and assess the contributions of each group member to the project. Unless a group reported an imbalance in its members' contributions, Peggy planned to assign a single project grade to all the members of the group.

In the first, narrative unit of the course, one student—Matt Wentz—turned in an account of his experience growing up with an alcoholic father. After reading a few paragraphs of this paper, Peggy immediately suspected it was plagiarized, so powerful and moving was the piece next to Matt's short assignments, which were poorly written and betrayed a general lack of sophisticated thinking. In an early informal assignment that asked the students to discuss their feelings about writing, Matt had confessed to disliking composition and to having struggled in most of his high school English courses. "I guess writing just isn't my bag," he wrote. As Peggy glanced back through Matt's rough in-process material, she noticed that Matt's early drafts showed only minor changes up to the final piece. His brainstorming notes, however, seemed a genuine conceptual exploration of what appeared in the paper. Thus, although Peggy had no evidence that Matt had plagiarized the paper, she decided to discuss its sophisticated style and ideas with him in a private conference.

The meeting was a disaster. At first Peggy tried not to accuse Matt or even suggest that she thought the paper was plagiarized, but simply to understand how Matt's style and ability could have changed so dramatically in just a few days. Yet Matt became immediately defiant and defensive. Sensing Matt's anger and feeling a little intimidated by his large figure, Peggy began backpedaling. "I just wanted to wait until I had a chance to discuss this with you before I assigned it a grade," Peggy said, realizing the meeting was going nowhere. "Look," Matt replied, almost thrusting his paper toward Peggy, "if you think I ripped this off—and I know you do—prove it. And if you still don't believe me, come on over to my parents' house sometime before dinner and have a couple of Scotches with my dad." Then he stormed out of the office.

Concerned about the apparent discrepancy between Matt's early assignments and this first major paper, yet lacking any proof that Matt had borrowed its language from some other source such as the files of papers and old exams at Matt's campus fraternity, Peggy decided reluctantly to give Matt's narrative the *A* it deserved (as a text) and wait to see what he would do on his next assignment.

During the unit, Peggy circulated among the groups, giving support and advice, answering questions, reading draft material, and even, on request, providing some written comments on sections of some groups' papers. Each time she tried to join Matt's group, however, she felt an air of tension, as if her presence somehow shut down their participation. Once she left, the group (the only all-male one in the class) would soon resume its chummy, almost boisterous interaction.

Over the two weeks of the session, Peggy felt herself less and less drawn to Matt's group and tried to cover her avoidance by seeming to become more immersed in the problems of other groups. At one point, interrupting the class to make a few important remarks, she noticed how three members of Matt's group sat almost scowling at her, their arms folded over their chests, although one of the members, Bob Webber, seemed his usual friendly self, fully engaged in Peggy's short presentation. Nevertheless, she came away from the class agitated, suspecting that Matt had somehow worked his will on the rest of the group and alienated them from her as a teacher.

After two weeks of hard group work, the class turned in the final drafts of their collaborative papers. Now, the papers in front of her, Peggy was interested to see what sort of project Matt's group had submitted. She glanced at the title, shaking her head: "Untitled Environment Article." The group had focused on the problem of deforestation by the timber industry in the Northwest. The first section seemed capably written but oddly void of any documentation, even though the details (especially some facts and figures) must have been extracted from some other source. Reading on, Peggy sensed something else, a kind of stylistic echo of a document she had read before. As she continued working her way through the first few pages, it slowly dawned on her that she was hearing bits and pieces of an article on endangered owl species in Oregon which she saw in an issue of *Time* a year or two before.

The next day, she managed to locate the issue she remembered and found the article, "Owl vs. Man." Glancing over the first paragraph, she was instantly struck by the similarity in style of the two documents. By the end of the first page, she had already located a block of four lines almost identical in wording to a passage from Matt's paper:

> None among these creatures is more vulnerable than the northern spotted owl, a bird so docile it will descend from the safety of its lofty bough to take a mouse from the hand of a man. (*Time,* June 25, 1990, p. 56)

> This bird, that is so docile it will come down from the protection of the high trees to grab a mouse from a man's hand, is becoming a menace to loggers. (Matt's group's paper, p. 2)

A quick reading of the paper side by side with the *Time* article convinced Peggy that Matt's group had plagiarized from at least this one piece, and possibly from several others as well, with no attempt at proper documentation.

When Peggy turned to the group's "process overview," she read the following short paragraph, insufficient in terms of her requirement that each group explain in detail the nature of their individual contributions:

> Process Overview
> Written by Bob Webber for the Group
> We all worked on this paper together, no-one did more than the other. We wrote small sections and then brought them into class and tryed to decide where they should be fused together. We made copies of all the articles for all of us and then worked on the pieces we had written, separately. This way the paper involved all of us equally.

When Peggy returned to the paper to conduct a more careful comparison with the *Time* article, she found that almost all of the plagiarized excerpts appeared in the first two and a half pages of the paper. The rest, while in a similar style and level of detail, clearly did not borrow from the article.

ISSUES FOR DISCUSSION

• Matt's group provided a written testimonial that they all had contributed equally to the project and presumably stood collectively behind it. Should Peggy confront any or all of the group members? If so, how should she proceed? Should she convene a group meeting or talk with each member individually? Easily intimidated, how should she handle the meeting?

• Peggy sensed that only one member of Matt's group, Bob Webber, decided not to oppose her instructionally. Should Peggy act on these feelings? Should she, for example, try to talk with Bob first, before confronting Matt or the others?

• How serious is the form of plagiarism evident in the paper? Given Peggy's situation, should she be concerned that this might be a case of simple ignorance rather than the willful theft of material from a copyrighted text?

• What would you advise Peggy about using this method again? What potential political and interpersonal issues emerge from our culture's insistence on the individual ownership of texts? How does such a view sit with the recent emphasis on the process of collaborative writing and learning?

Behind a Closed Door

Ann Redwin was nervous about teaching her first introductory writing course. A twenty-two-year-old beginning graduate teaching assistant, she had been an excellent student as an undergraduate and had even won the departmental award as the outstanding graduating English major. She had done very well on her GRE, and, beginning graduate school, she felt well versed in the standard canon of English and American literature, sensitive to the structure and functions of language, and confident in her abilities as a writer. But this business of *teaching*— that was another matter completely.

Before getting her own class, Ann had enrolled in a workshop on pedagogy, had observed several classes like the one she would be assigned, and had even done some limited "practice" teaching herself. Still, she was worried about her ability to control the classroom situation. On the day before her class was to begin, she brought her concerns to the director of the program. "I don't know how to behave," Ann told the director. "One of my friends who's been teaching for years told me that I've got to come down hard on the students right from the beginning and let them know who's boss because the students will be constantly testing me to see what they can get away with. She told me I shouldn't even smile until midterm."

The director, a veteran of twenty-five years of undergraduate teaching, tried to reassure Ann, whom she recognized as a level-headed, bright, dependable person. "Just be yourself," the director said. "Treat your students like adult acquaintances. Smile if you're moved to smile, look distressed if you are. Just don't let the students know that you're scared and you think that because this is your first time teaching you expect to screw up every minute. Your students must see you as confident, poised, and in control."

Ann left the conference with her spirits buoyed, ready to begin the new term. The first two days of the class went beautifully: Ann felt completely in control, and her students responded by doing exactly what she wanted. On the first day, Ann went over the course syllabus and requirements and had the students write about their previous experiences in writing classes. On the second day, the students wrote an in-class essay in which they were to introduce themselves to one of their peers and speculate about their educational plans for the next four years. Ann told the students that she would read their papers that night and provide them with an initial assessment of their writing on the next class day. Maybe the first two sessions went so well because Ann had planned and conducted them well, but maybe they went well because Brian wasn't there.

Brian Holinger made a pretty spectacular entrance on the third day of the term. About ten minutes after class began, he appeared in the doorway and just stood there. "This section 24702?" he asked, glancing first at a piece of paper he was carrying and then around the room. "You Miss Ann Redwin?"

Ann said yes and signaled for him to come in and sit down. "Hi, kids. Hi, Annie," Brian sang out. He grinned at Ann, winked and made a kind of clicking sound, and moved to an open seat precisely in the middle of the room. Ann felt herself redden but continued with the class. She had returned the initial essays at the beginning of the hour, using a handout of examples from the students' papers, and was going over successful and not-so-successful passages. She gave Brian a handout and he read it over quickly, whistling softly and chuckling occasionally. Then, as Ann worked with each example, Brian would utter, *sotto voce* but loud enough for everyone to hear, comments like "You gotta be kidding me" and "That's pretty lame, isn't it." Soon the class was far more fixed on Brian's responses than on Ann's instruction.

With about ten minutes left in the class, Ann finished going over the handout and Brian's hand shot up. He wondered, he said, whether he could introduce himself to the class since he hadn't had the opportunity to write one of these introductory essays. "Well, I suppose," Ann uttered, and Brian in a flash was standing behind the podium.

He launched into a spirited narrative about how he had enlisted in the army right out of high school, how he had become the star recruit in basic training, how he had passed his tour of duty largely "gittin' drunk and shootin' pool." He had the class eating out of his hand, and he timed his peroration perfectly, declaring just as the bell rang that he had spent "six of the best years of my life protectin' democracy for you co-eds and frat boys, and now at the ripe age of twenty-four I'm gonna become one of you."

The next week was pure hell for Ann. Brian wisecracked his way through Ann's lecture on the purposes and modes of writing on Monday, through her exercises on prewriting techniques on Wednesday, and through her discussion of a model essay on Friday. He was so quick-witted that the other students would turn in his direction at the slightest pause in the class to catch his show. Ann tried to ignore the problem and did her best to call on all the students to contribute except Brian, who constantly had his hand in the air. More than once, when a student did not respond to Ann's prompt, a group of students in the back row would say in unison, "Well, Brian?" and there would be a torrent of laughter.

Late Friday afternoon, Ann once again came to the director of the program for help. Describing the situation vividly, Ann cried out, "What can I do? He's got control of my class." The director saw nothing to be gained from confronting Brian in front of the class. That would simply give him the audience he wanted, and certainly Ann would have a difficult time keeping her cool in such a confrontation. "Ask to see him in your office hours," the director said, "and speak to him as one adult to another. Tell him that his constantly clowning around is distracting to the class and nobody profits from it. Don't get mad—just be firm with him."

The following Monday Brian was up to his typical hi-jinks, but after class Ann asked him to see her in her office one hour later. He complied and arrived precisely on time. Ann asked him to come in and sit down, and she shut the door. She laid out the situation to Brian exactly as the director had recommended. Brian was a model of humility. He blushed slightly and looking at his shoes muttered that he was sorry. "Sometimes I guess I'm pretty full of it." Ann accepted the apology and told him that she would see him on Wednesday. "From now on, we'll work together," he said on the way out.

The turnabout in the class was amazing. Brian's wisecracks were gone. When students looked at him for response, he simply looked down to his notebook or ahead to Ann in the front of the room. After a couple days without the jokes, Ann felt she could call on Brian to respond in a class discussion. He did so seriously, intelligently, and calmly. Whereas previously he had captured the students' attention with his clowning, now he was becoming the model student. As the fourth week of the term ended, Ann congratulated herself on how well the class was proceeding. Most of the students were conscientious: they attended regularly, did their homework, and participated in the class. On that Friday, they had just handed in their second formal essay for the term.

At about three o'clock that afternoon, Ann was sitting alone in her office. She intended to leave about an hour later, so she thought she would read quickly through as many of her students' papers as she could. She had just gotten started when Brian showed up at her door.

"Uh, I wonder if I could talk to you about the paper I just handed in," he asked in a hushed voice.

"Sure," Ann said, "I haven't gotten to yours yet, but if you have a seat, I'll look at it right now."

Without a word, Brian sat in a chair beside her desk. She leafed through the stack, found his essay, and began reading. Quickly, a lump formed in her throat and she began to feel herself redden again. The essay was a story about a twenty-four-year-old army veteran college freshman who falls in love with his composition instructor, "a beautiful, twenty-two-year-old brain who showed me how to be a man."

Ann looked up from the paper in disbelief. Brian put one hand on top of hers and said huskily, "What do you say let's go have a beer. I'd really like to talk to you about how I feel."

ISSUES FOR DISCUSSION

• What should Ann do at the very minute the scenario ends?

• Did the director of the program give Ann good advice at the beginning of the term, when Ann came to her initially? What about the second time, when she counseled Ann to confront Brian directly but privately?

• If this incident were to happen on your campus, should somebody be told about it? Who?

• To what extent does the situation described in this scenario bother you?

6 Teaching Writing:
Course Designs

Designing a writing course is an interesting, even exciting enterprise, but there are so many possibilities that teachers sometimes feel overwhelmed. Adopting a textbook and basing course organization on its chapter sequence is a common, quick way to arrive at a design, but that solution is less adequate than it looks, and it brings some hazards too.

The word *textbook* is used here to refer to what are commonly called "rhetorics" or "guides to writing well"—books organized by stages of the writing process or by rhetorical purposes or features or techniques. Of course two other kinds of books are often used in writing courses, namely, reference handbooks and books of readings. But handbooks are not intended as a basis for course organization, and although books of readings can assume that role, they function as organizers only at a high level of abstraction—typically by grouping readings under a theme. It is primarily "rhetorics" or "guides"—books about writing—that appear to offer definite guidance on course aims and organization. Yet these are the books most likely to displace students' own writing as the center of study in a writing course.

Such a displacement may be fine if a teacher believes that writing courses should focus on information *about* writing, but increasingly, teachers are primarily concerned with engaging students *in* writing. Textbooks often inadvertently limit students' engagement because they cannot deal with specific, dynamic issues of content and purpose. Textbooks can help students gain perspective on rhetoric as a field, and they can organize strategic information efficiently, but they can also inhibit students' use of writing as a tool of inquiry.

The importance of this engagement in writing will depend on a teacher's purposes. Some courses will focus on writing as a means of participation in a social or disciplinary context; others will stress expression of the self. Some will focus on the generation of ideas; in others the final text will be the central concern. Some set of answers to basic questions about the aims of writing instruction will be present in every course and in every textbook. Explicit aims may not appear to vary a lot but implicit aims do, and assumed relations between strategies and aims vary even more. To make a well-based choice among textbooks, a teacher must think through course design issues much as she would need to do if she were not going to rely on a text at all.

The numbers and kinds of books produced for writing courses force another humbling recognition: no one course can fully realize all the values potentially addressed by writing instruction. Any course may well foster some values directly and others indirectly, but decisions about focus do have to be made and courses designed accordingly.

The most basic decisions concern the students' sense of their writing purpose. Traditional labels like "exposition" and "argumentation," "description" and "narration" usually imply that modes are purposes, but obviously they are not. Defining purposes by naming modes or forms invites students to see composition as mere exercise, rehearsal for future "real" occasions when they will actually need to write. Defining purposes by asking students to answer questions that appear to be open but really are not—questions intended only to elicit recitation that is intellectually and ideologically correct—is even more alienating. *Creating credible occasions for writing from which well-defined purposes can emerge: that is the essential aim of good course design.* Two key questions must be considered together: What should students write about? And why (which is partly for whom) should they write?

The scenarios in this chapter consist of several syllabi and course descriptions, together with statements of each instructor's goals and philosophy. All the designs are for courses that university students might take during their first year, but they are not equally general; that is, the courses make different assumptions about what student writers need to learn, what approaches aid learning, and how what is learned will be integrated.

A Personal Essay Course

Gary Lawrence believes that a writing course should help students cultivate a distinctive voice. For Gary, academic prose tends to stifle students' voices, alienate them from their own experiences, and promote a narrow vocationalism at odds with the fundamental aims of liberal education. He will therefore not ask his students for academic essays, but instead for personal essays addressed to a general audience. By writing such essays, his students will be learning to produce what Gary considers the generic qualities of good writing.

Students will learn to recognize good writing, and so to define their own aims, by reading essays—complex, personal reflections—by professional writers. The professionals' essays will demonstrate what it means to think critically about one's personal experiences and, more broadly, about one's culture. The text for the course will be *Eight Modern Essayists,* edited by William Smart. Excerpts from Gary's syllabus follow. He planned for a ten-week course.

Writing Requirements

1. A journal for reflections on course readings and for observations and memories—ideas for essays to be written. Some entries will be assigned, others left open to choice. Entries should average 3 pages per week; a minimum of 25 journal pages will be required for the quarter. Journals will be collected twice and returned with comments.

2. The outline for a group presentation on one of the writers in the course text and a two-page summary of material delivered as a talk, i.e., one segment of what the group presents. The class will be divided into five or six groups to study essayists not already scheduled to be discussed in connection with essay assignments. Groups will need to choose among Woolf, Orwell, Thomas, Didion, and—if they are prepared to do outside reading—the writers represented by just one essay in our course text. Groups will study writers' choices of subjects, the ways writers relate to their subjects and to their readers, and the images writers create of themselves. They will analyze sentences, paragraphs, and whole essays in order to explain what characterizes each writer's style and offer examples to show what creates particular stylistic effects. An important part of each group presentation will be journal assignments developed by the group, to be addressed by the rest of the class.

3. Three essays, five-six pages long, two drafts (preliminary and final) to be submitted for each. The assignments follow.

A. Having studied E. B. White's essays "On a Florida Key" and "Death of a Pig," use them as a kind of model. Choose one of these two options:

* Describe a place that is interesting or meaningful to you.

* Narrate an important event in your life.

  What you think of "interesting" or "meaningful" or "important" will not necessarily have been conspicuous—those who know you may not have realized that, for you, a place or an event was significant, or they may have made the wrong assumptions about why it was significant. Your essay should bring readers close, help them experience as you did the place or event that you write about.

B. Respond to Carol Bly's "Growing Up Expressive." Choose one of these two options:

* You can narrate an episode from your own school experience so that, by implication, you affirm and illustrate Bly's point or call her point into question.

* You can directly, explicitly argue for or against what Bly says: Do you agree with her that "the problem-solving mentality" is pervasive and unfortunate? Do you think schools should resist it and "educate children to be madly expressive all their lives"?

C. Choose one of these two options:

* In "The Civil Rights Movement: What Good Was It?" Alice Walker makes a strong connection between public events and her personal life. Some of her concerns when she wrote the essay in 1967 would probably not play a role if she were writing it today, but she might well use some of the same material and make the same general point.

An essay you write in 1991 connecting a public movement or event with your own life will probably be similar to Walker's in that way. Feel free to discuss whatever seems relevant now, even though some things will probably become dated as Walker's reference to the rarity of black hippies has. But do think hard about what your key point will be—that should not date so easily. Walker's key point is the answer to the question that titles her essay, and it is still powerful. Aim for that kind of power—a connection between your life and a public movement or event that will still interest you and your readers twenty years from now.

* A student reacting to Paul Fussell's "Appearance Counts" said, "I hate that essay. I don't want to believe Fussell, but I haven't been able to figure out where he is wrong." What do you think of Fussell's essay? Write a response to the student quoted here, explaining either why you too dislike the essay, or why, instead, you like it. To prepare, you need to consider what makes an essay good and what makes an essay likable. Are they the same, or always the same, or the same for every reader? Examine both the point of the essay and the ways the point is made, and watch for shifts in tone.

Whether you attack or defend Fussell's essay, be sure to treat it with respect. That means, among other things, that you must study this long essay carefully, so you don't seem to choose details arbitrarily as a basis for praise or blame. You need a grasp of the essay as a whole, and you should think hard about why "Appearance Counts" is more likely than most essays in our collection to provoke a strongly judgmental response.

Class Calendar

Week 1

In-class writing: Students' experiences as writers, and their ideas about what makes writing good.

Class discussion: Issues raised by writing done in class. A writer's role; the nature of the personal essay.

Reading assignment: Essays by E. B. White, Weeks 1 and 2.

Journal assignments: Write a short paragraph on your first reaction to "Once More to the Lake." Write again about your reaction after reading the essay a second time. Write a third time after class discussion of this essay. Has your view of it changed in any important way? Follow the same sequence to make entries on "The Death of a Pig."

Week 2

Journal assignments:

a. Set aside an Essay I section in your journal—at least five pages. Jot down ideas for events and places you might want to write about. List ideas separately and leave spaces. Come back to your ideas page every day or so to add, discard, and relate possibilities.

b. What do you think "The Death of a Pig" is really about—besides the death of a pig? How can you tell? One-page entry.

c. Consider all four of White's essays: What kind of thing interests him? Do the subjects of these essays have anything in common? One to two pages.

d. Choose a sentence you think is especially effective from one of White's essays, and explain what creates its special effect—up to one page.

Class discussion: E. B. White's essays. Ideas for first essay.

Conferences: 10-minute meeting with instructor to discuss possibilities for first essay.

Week 3

Due: Draft of first essay.

Two-day workshop: Peer groups meet to discuss drafts. When the workshop ends, writers collect response sheets from their peer groups and write one-page reflective statements explaining which responses were useful. Response sheets and reflective statements are to be turned in to the instructor on the day when regular full class meetings resume.

Class discussion: Common problems in drafts—recognizing, prioritizing, solving.

Planning for group presentations: Groups studying essays by Thomas and Didion will need to present in Week 5. Groups on Woolf, Orwell, and any other writers will present in Week 9.

Week 4

Due: Final version of first essay.

Class discussion: First essay, selected papers.

Reading assignment: Essays by Carol Bly.

Conferences with instructor for groups working on Thomas and Didion to prepare for presentations.

Week 5

Journal assignments:

a. Choose a paragraph by Carol Bly that attracts your attention and analyze its structure—one page.

b. Identify key words in one of Bly's essays and explain how they function—why they are "key."

Class discussion: Carol Bly's essays.

Group presentations on Thomas and Didion.

Journals due.

[The remainder of the calendar is abbreviated. Journal entries, for example, continue.]

Week 6

Due: Draft of second essay.

Two-day workshop.

Class discussion: Excerpts from journals.

Journals returned.

Week 7

Due: Final version of second essay.

Class discussion: Essays by Paul Fussell.

Week 8

Class discussion: Essays by Alice Walker.

Due at the end of the week: Draft of third essay.

Week 9

Two-day class workshop.

Group presentations of Woolf and Orwell.

Week 10

Due: Final version of third essay.

Group presentations on other writers.

Due: Journals.

ISSUES FOR DISCUSSION

• After submitting the first essay, two students tell Gary Lawrence that they are worried because they do not see much connection between their writing course work and the writing they must do in their history and anthropology courses. What differences between these situations should Gary acknowledge, if any? How defensible is Gary's course premise that good writing is generic? Should he stress that writing courses are intended to help students gain confidence in their own voices? Should he say that learning to write for a general audience naturally (or necessarily) comes first? Should he emphasize that students will find that examining their personal experience by writing is valuable for its own sake? Are there other responses he might make? How compelling do you find the various possible responses?

• The editor of *Eight Modern Essayists* says that concentrating on a few good writers can help students learn to write, and Gary entirely agrees. But the editor goes on to say that the purpose of reading the essays is not to learn devices or stratagems used by successful writers, and that makes Gary feel a little uneasy, perhaps disloyal, because he asks students to identify rhetorical devices and stylistic stratagems and discuss them in their journals. Is there something wrong with this approach? The editor makes only one positive reference to what *should* be done in order to learn from the collected essays: he says he has chosen only essays "worth studying in depth." What would constitute studying "in depth"? What questions should be raised? Do any or all of the assigned questions for journal entries and group presentations seem appropriate? What are the most important things Gary should expect his students to learn from the essays?

• Gary's three essay assignments make several kinds of personal and intellectual demands. Is any assignment likely to be too easy or too difficult? Should the assignments be more alike? Will students see the first assignment, essentially to write a description or a narrative, as a request merely to demonstrate a form? Gary is counting on E. B. White's example to keep the students from seeing the assignment this way. Is he being realistic? What sense of purpose should the students recognize in White and develop in their own writing? Assignments two and three offer the option of writing straightforward arguments. Will such responses qualify as personal essays? Will some but not others? Does it matter?

• When the students meet in small groups to discuss drafts of their essays, they read the drafts aloud twice, but do not provide printed copies for each other. Gary instructs them simply to listen, carefully, to the first reading. A few moments are allowed for jotting down general impressions and high points when the reading is completed; then the second reading begins. This time, group members note specific reactions as the reading proceeds, using a sheet with three columns marked +, −, and ?. After the second reading is completed, group members explain their responses, and the writer simply takes all comments under advisement. The comments are intended, of course, to aid revision, but enthusiasm for the group readings is mixed. Getting productive responses from peer groups takes work in any kind of writing course, but each kind of course presents particular problems and opportunities. How would the students' writing purpose in Gary's course be likely to affect peer group response? What about the essay assignments—what response issues are each likely to raise? Would you suggest any changes in the reading group procedures?

• Should Gary have conferences with students on their drafts? How might that affect his workload? Should something be cut? What kinds of preparation will Gary need in order to use students' writing in class? What criteria should guide his selection of essays, essay excerpts, and journal entries for class discussion? How should he structure discussion of students' work in class?

• Gary's colleague, Josephine Pedroza, agrees that focusing on the personal essay is appropriate, but she wants to be sure that her students learn some basics about thesis sentences, essay organization, and so on. She likes *Eight Modern Essayists,* but the rich essays in this collection are not easy to use as models for structure because they are so complex; in fact, many do not even have an explicit thesis. She decides that asking her students to see them as models and to write personal essays themselves would be asking for trouble: she is not comfortable commenting on and evaluating essays when the criteria for good performance are likely to seem unstable, and she wants to be sure that students realize they are learning broadly useful writing techniques. So Josephine makes analytical essay assignments: her students produce written analyses of professionals' personal essays. Josephine requires her students to buy another text for the course, *The Random House Handbook* (Crews), and she assigns passages in it every week. She also hands out vocabulary lists as preparation for discussing particular essays, and she gives an occasional vocabulary quiz. Below is a sample from her calendar.

Week 2

Eight Modern Essayists (EME), p. 80-93 (two essays by E. B. White)

Random House Handbook (RHH), p. 29-32; 74-82 (finding a thesis; supplying evidence)

Assignment for Essay I: Analyze one of the remaining E. B. White essays, p. 94-103. Draft will be due Monday of Week 4.

Week 3

EME, p. 111-124 (five essays by Lewis Thomas)

RHH, p. 161-173; 141-145 (paragraph development; conciseness and variety)

Vocabulary list on Thomas's essays.

• Is Josephine's course an improvement over Gary's? Would that judgment depend on the students' level of sophistication? Should the *Handbook* assignments be discussed in class? If not, will the students read them? If they are discussed, will they weaken course continuity based on the reading of professionals' essays? How are the issues raised by the *Handbook* best integrated into the course?

• Another colleague, Monique Carter, accepts Gary's reasons for focusing on the personal essay, but she rejects *Eight Modern Essayists*— in fact, she decides not to use professional essays in her course at all. She thinks putting any sort of text on a pedestal is ideologically naïve. Furthermore, as a practical matter, she is skeptical about students' ability to use the essays in *EME* as models. At best, she thinks students will be intimidated by the work of skilled, older, professional writers.

The problem for Monique is to find ways of pushing her students, encouraging them to make appropriately ambitious demands on themselves. (She does not want to read strings of clichés on tired topics.) She thinks that a carefully designed assignment sequence might be the answer, but she knows that developing such a sequence will take a lot of time. She considers using William Coles's sequence described in *Teaching Composition*, but is worried that it would control the students' work so much that many values she associates with personal essays would be lost.

Is Monique right to reject *Eight Modern Essayists* as a text, or to reject professional essays as models generally? Can an assignment sequence without model readings provide appropriate amounts of freedom and constraint for students writing personal essays? What could a suitable sequence be based on?

• How would you compare these three approaches—Gary's, Josephine's, and Monique's?

A Forms and Strategies Course

Mark Burregg, a twenty-four-year-old teaching assistant who is pursuing a doctorate in applied linguistics, teaches writing in a program that has "unit adoptions" of textbooks and a common curriculum: a committee of administrators and instructors designs the curriculum and chooses a common textbook that must be used in all sections of a course.

Mark believes strongly in the curriculum and the textbook of choice. He sees the introductory college writing course as a "service course"— that it should (1) teach students how to produce clear and correct prose so that they can succeed in their other university course work, and (2) provide them with what Mark calls "specific intellectual and organizational strategies" that they will be called upon to perform and apply in their studies. Mark, who is beginning his third year as a teacher of college writing, has generally found that his students have had lots of experience in their previous schooling with two kinds of writing: personal writing, in which they have been asked to describe scenes that were vivid in their imaginations, narrate meaningful incidents from their past, or tell stories that taught them some moral or ethical point; and literary critical writing, in which they have written about themes, characters, and other features of poems, short stories, novels, and plays. Mark sees these kinds of writing as relatively useless for college students: unless they intend to become freelance journalists or English majors, he reasons, students will not be required to write personally or criticize imaginative literature regularly. This, he maintains, is not the kind of writing that people must do in the humanities, the social and "hard" sciences, and the technological fields.

In Mark's course, the students will practice six major strategies: defining, serializing, classifying, summarizing, comparing, and analyzing. They will apply these strategies individually in essays about challenging academic subjects, much like those they encounter in their classes throughout the curriculum. They will conclude the term by writing a major paper that uses several of these strategies. The text for the course will be *Critical Strategies for Academic Writing,* by Malcolm Kiniry and Mike Rose. Portions of Mark's syllabus follow.

Writing Assignments

1. You will write three 2- to 4-page papers, one each demonstrating the strategies of defining, serializing, and classifying.

2. You will write three 3- to 5-page papers, one each demonstrating the strategies of summarizing, comparing, and analyzing.

3. You will write one 8- to 10-page paper demonstrating several of these strategies. As part of the requirement for this paper, you will keep a process log (see below) and a one-page overview of the assignment, explaining which of the strategies you were using and how you were trying to use them.

4. You will be assigned to a four-member writing group. In the group, you will be required at four times during the semester to present your draft for constructive critique by the other group members. Here is how the rotation will work:

Paper 1: Defining—Students A and B will present drafts.

Paper 2: Serializing—Students C and D will present drafts.

Paper 3: Classifying—Students A and B will present drafts.

Paper 4: Summarizing—Students C and D will present drafts.
Paper 5: Comparing—Students A and B will present drafts.
Paper 6: Analyzing—Students C and D will present drafts.
Paper 7: Final paper—All four students will present drafts.

I expect you to accomplish your group critiques as out-of-class homework, and I will ask you to turn in copies of your drafts and response notes as evidence that your writing group has met.

Since Mark intended to work through the Kiniry and Rose text sequentially, he decided not to list daily assignments on the syllabus. Instead, for the first eleven weeks of the semester, he directed the students to read all the material in the first two sections of each chapter—the "general considerations" and the demonstrative cases—for the first day of the period designated for covering each strategy. On successive days, he assigns specific brief sections from the "first passes" to be started in class, completed as homework, and discussed in following sessions. He also reserves the right to discuss specific issues of organization, style, usage, and mechanics as they arise in students' papers.

Class Calendar

Weeks 1 & 2:   Defining
Weeks 3 & 4:   Serializing
Weeks 5 & 6:   Classifying
Week 7:   Summarizing
Weeks 8 & 9:   Comparing
Weeks 10 & 11:   Analyzing

During the final four weeks, students will work on their longer papers. During weeks 12 and 13, Mark demonstrates major principles of writing from sources. During week 14, he will cancel classes to have individual conferences with students about their papers. At the beginning of week 15, he will conduct workshops on revising longer papers written from sources. The final papers are due at the end of week 15. There is no final examination.

Each of the first six assignments emerges directly from the pedagogy in the Kiniry and Rose textbook; indeed, its first six chapters are entitled "Defining," "Serializing," "Classifying," "Summarizing," "Comparing," and "Analyzing." Each chapter follows the same pattern: the authors briefly introduce the strategy and explain where students might have to employ it in their studies. Next, they "walk through" the strategy, demonstrating it by using subject matter from different disciplines. Then they offer brief assignments called "first passes" that allow students to practice the strategy on their own. Finally, they present longer reading-and-writing assignments, with many options from different academic fields, that call for students to write papers demonstrating the strategy. Below are thumbnail sketches of these assignments that Mark includes in his syllabus:

Assignments 1-6

1. Defining—Following Kiniry and Rose's model using the word assassin, read the Oxford English Dictionary definitions of chauvinism, cybernetics, evolve, and technology and write your own definition of one of these terms, drawing on the OED's historical information. Two to four pages.

2. Serializing—From a passage from Science Fiction: History, Science, Vision, by Robert Scholes and Eric Rabkin, adapt information to produce a chronological account of the development of evolutionary theory from the time of Lamarck through the work of Hugo De Vries in 1900. Two to four pages.

3. Classifying—After reading the opening paragraphs of 31 works of nonfiction prose, write an essay classifying and illustrasting the methods such writers use to introduce their work. Two to four pages.

4. Summarizing—After reading a 13-paragraph passage from Homeboys: Gangs, Drugs, and Prison in the Barrios of Los Angeles, by Joan Moore, write a one-paragraph summary of the passage and then respond to the following questions from the Kiniry and Rose textbook: "What does Moore see as original about her approach to the subject of the barrio economy? What are the advantages of her approach?" Three to five pages.

5. Comparing—After reading passages from Benjamin Franklin's Autobiography and The Autobiography of Malcolm X, write an essay comparing the two authors' involvement with reading. Three to five pages.

6. Analyzing—After reading a passage on four phases of culture shock, read the accounts of coming to America by three writers—Mary Antin, Maxine Hong Kingston, and Wood Chuen Kwong—and write an essay analyzing the culture shock experienced by these three people. Three to five pages.

For their longer paper, the students will be able to choose from two sets of thematically organized materials that the textbook presents in its second half, entitled "Readings for Academic Argument: A Sourcebook." They may choose to read fifteen selections on the issue of "Women and Power: Perspectives from Anthropology" and write a paper in response to this prompt: "Support or argue against the idea that modern industrial societies have widened the differences between women and men." Or the students may choose to read sixteen selections, including a historical array of cartoons, on the subject of "What's Funny? Investigating the Comic" and write a paper in response to this prompt: "'All laughter is aggression. Comedy is cruel.' Support or dispute this claim with a well-developed argument." Whichever option they choose, the students are expected to write an eight- to ten-page paper drawing on their own ideas and experiences and on specific issues and material from the readings. When they turn in their final draft of this paper, the students must also submit a one-page explanation of how they tried to employ the six critical strategies. They must also submit a log of their writing processes, using Mark's guide:

Process Log

Write at least a complete sentence (no sentence fragments, please!), but no more than a paragraph, in response to each of the following questions:

1. Did you know much about this topic before you wrote this paper? What did you know?

2. Why did you choose the title for the paper? Did you have other titles that you decided not to use? What were they?

3. Did your ideas about the topic change while you were working on the paper? If so, how did they change?

4. Which passage in the paper—it could be a single sentence or as much as a couple of paragraphs—do you think represents your best writing style?

5. Which passage in the paper—again, it could be a single sentence or as much as a couple of paragraphs—did you have to work on in a concentrated fashion to get the style appropriate and correct?

6. What are the three most important changes from previous drafts that you made in the revised, polished version? Why did you make those changes?

7. What one aspect of "housecleaning"—spelling, usage, mechanics, and punctuation—did you really concentrate on perfecting in the revised, polished version? Give a specific example of this aspect.

8. Choose one person you talked to before or during the writing of the paper. What did you talk about? What effect did it have on your paper?

9. In the process of writing this paper, did you do anything different from what you have done when writing papers in the past? What was it?

10. When did you receive the initial assignment that eventually led to this paper? Between the time you received the assignment and the time you handed in the revised, polished version, when did you do the most work on this paper? Where

did you work on it most of the time? Describe the environment of this space. Estimate the total amount of time you
spent working on the paper, including planning, drafting, discussing, revising, editing, and typing.

11. If you could spend another half an hour on this paper,
what would you do?

ISSUES FOR DISCUSSION

• Very early in the course, Mark begins to hear students grumbling
about the subject matter of their reading and writing assignments, and
finally in week 3 one student is bold enough to speak up in class. "A
lot of us have been talking about this stuff you want us to read and
write about, and we don't like it. We don't know anything about the
earth's water movement or barter economies or endocytosis and exo-
cytosis or the nuclear arms race, and you expect us to come to class
every day and read and write about these things? Why can't we write
about whatever we want to? All our other teachers have always let us
choose our own subjects, stuff we knew about. Why can't we do that
here?" How should Mark respond to these complaints?

• Once he gets his first set of papers, Mark decides he needs to
supplement the Kiniry and Rose text with other materials, perhaps
including a handbook of some sort that he can direct students to
consult about issues of process, organization, sentence structure, style,
diction, usage, and punctuation. Would you also feel the need to
supplement a course like Mark's with other materials? If so, what
kinds?

• Within the first few weeks of the class, Mark notices that many of
his students' papers, both their in-class work and the drafts of their
out-of-class papers, read more like responses to essay questions on
exams than self-sufficient, independent compositions. Should Mark be
surprised by this discovery? Should he try to get his students to write
differently?

• About five weeks into the course, a student comes to see Mark
during office hours. "I'm afraid I'm really screwing up the classifying
assignment," the student says. "I'm really trying to say something
distinctive about these authors' methods of introducing their essays,
but I feel like all I'm doing is saying in my own words what they've
already said in the pieces in the book. Isn't that serializing? Weren't
we supposed to be done with that last week? Or is it summarizing, and
we're not supposed to get to that until week 7, are we?" In week 9,
another student comes to see Mark with a similar concern. "I'm

working on my paper comparing Franklin's and Malcolm's attitudes about reading, and I find that all I'm doing is summarizing instead. Am I doing this assignment all wrong?" What kind of advice and instruction should Mark provide to these students?

• About halfway through the semester, Mark is in his office reading his students' papers when his office mate, another young instructor, picks up several and begins reading them. "I hate to say this, Mark, but your students' papers are really stiff. I mean, there's no humanity to them—there's no sense of voice and personality. I mean, look at this one," she says, tossing it toward him. "It reads like a parody of an academic journal article."

Mark is annoyed at her offering this unsolicited opinion, but he takes a look at the paper and realizes she is right. In many of the papers—about 30 to 40 percent of them—the students are writing extremely long, loose sentences, overusing *be* verbs, employing long nominalizations, relying almost completely on passive verb constructions—all the symptoms, he thinks, of deadly academic prose. What do you think might be the cause of such lifelessness? Is it possible to write "academic prose" that is not lifeless?

• Mark has great confidence in the basic pedagogical premise of his class, namely, that if students can read and identify what Kiniry and Rose call "critical strategies" in professional texts, they will be able to use those strategies in their own writing. Discuss this assumption.

A Thematic Writing Course

Don Jackson has just finished his graduate degree in English and has taken his first full-time college teaching position. It requires that he teach two sections of introductory composition each term, along with one introductory literature course and one upper-division course. Don taught composition while he was a teaching assistant, and although he never had the opportunity to design his own course (the university where he studied required TAs to follow a common syllabus), he did develop some very distinct ideas about what a college writing course should be and do.

Don's new university has no set syllabus, and faculty members are permitted to teach composition in any way they see fit. But before teaching his new sections, Don was asked to give a copy of his syllabus to the department's composition committee and accompany it with a memo justifying his curriculum and pedagogy. Part of his memo consisted of the following statement:

Five Key Ideas Underlying My Course

1. There is no such thing as a content-free writing course. Students in college writing courses must read and write about something. One learns about writing—and to write effectively—by engaging in a sustained inquiry on a single subject, or a set of related subjects, over an extended period. By doing so, students learn the nature of writing as an intellectual activity—and that is what really transfers from their composition course to their courses in the remainder of the university curriculum. What transfers is not any notion of context-free invention heuristics, or generic formats for papers, or principles of sentence structure, diction, or usage. What transfers is that people learn by writing—it is through writing about what one is studying that one really learns.

2. Students in college writing courses ought to be exposed to a wide variety of prose forms: literary essays, scholarly studies, articles from the popular press, and so on. Students should see that each of these genres represents a certain community's way of learning—its way of responding to intellectual questions and adding to an intellectual conversation on an issue.

3. Just as practicing scholars have a research program that allows them to write up their scholarship in sequence—one article leads to the next, which leads to the next, and so on— so should students in college writing courses be taught a notion of sequencing. Their essays should not be isolated entities, each beginning de novo, but instead should exist in a sequence where the first essay leads to the second, and these lead to a third, and so on.

4. Students in college writing courses should learn the different purposes that writing serves. In their high school writing experiences, students generally have written only for one purpose: to demonstrate to some teacher/reader/examiner that they know the "correct" answer to some question. High school student writers accomplish this purpose when they write themes about literature, simply spouting back "what the teacher said the book was about"; similarly, they accomplish this purpose when they write essay exams about "the four causes of the Civil War" or book reports that masquerade as research papers. I want students in my college writing course to write in order to clarify issues for themselves, to inform readers on subject matters that the readers don't know about already, to explore their subject and raise numerous questions about it, to convince readers to believe in the writer's thesis, and to change the ways people typically think and act about a subject at hand.

5. The writing class is an intellectual community, embedded in the larger intellectual community of the university as a whole. Thus, the students and the instructor should engage in a

mutual, communal investigation of a subject and effective writing about it. This means that students are required to produce rough drafts, to have their drafts workshopped in whole class discussions, and to work weekly in writing groups; they are permitted to revise any essay as fully and as frequently as they'd like, and they are assessed via a portfolio of writing submitted at midterm and the end of the term.

Having laid out this rationale, Don explained that he wanted his students to work for the entire term on a sequence of four reading and writing assignments on a subject that he believed all college students would find challenging and engaging, specifically how individuals and societies define the concept of *self.* He wanted the students to investigate the self as an isolated entity, in relation to other people, in relation to one's work, and in relation to the government. He selected a group of extremely varied and often difficult readings, with authors ranging from Plato to Carson McCullers, and media ranging from *Mother Jones* to a papal encyclical. He very carefully wrote a sequence of four writing assignments, making sure to provide at least two options for each. He specifically hoped that assignment one would lead to two, one and two would lead to three, and so on. In other words, although his students were writing four projects, in essence he wanted them to see their work for the term as culminating in the final essay.

Here is the sequence Don developed:[1]

Boundaries of the Individual

This above all: to thine own self be true,
And it must follow, as the night the day,
Thou canst not then be false to any man.
                    Shakespeare, Hamlet

Be yourself. Know yourself. Think for yourself. These are some of the truisms that most of us have grown up with.

An elusive thing, the self. It is difficult to define, much less to find or act upon. You may finish this sequence asking, "Is the self even there?" To confront this difficult question, this sequence examines some of the ways people talk about the self.

Here in the United States, we often think of ourselves as a nation of individuals, pioneering new vistas in solitary effort. But how far does this individualism go? How important is it? Where does the self end and the rest of the world begin?

The amount of time we spend interacting with various organizations and structures in our society says something about the kind of individuals we are. The way we feel about work and government and how large a role they should play in our lives indicates our priorities and our philosophies of life. Should the individual self be recognized within the family? In the workplace? In government? How do different cultural or religious traditions affect the way we think about ourselves and the way we act?

Students often protest that asking questions like this is "just philosophical." It can seem of little value to write, often at great length, about what seems to be an abstract topic. But the answers to questions about the self are not merely an excuse to "be philosophical." Through this sequence of reading and writing assignments, you can see that the answers given throughout history have shaped our homes, our families, our educations, our occupations, our forms of government, and then, like a circle, our ideas about ourselves.

This sequence offers a chance to discover directly something about writing that is often frustrating, always difficult, but sometimes almost magical—a chance to discover a part of "thine own self."

ASSIGNMENT ONE

Readings: May Sarton, "The Rewards of Living a Solitary Life."

Carson McCullers, "Loneliness: An American Malady."

Margaret Mead, "Rage, Rhythm, and Autonomy."

"THE SELF"

Carson McCullers and May Sarton both seem to believe that a separation exists between the "self" and the world of others. McCullers thinks that what the human struggle is all about is the need to lose our sense of isolated identity so that we might "belong to something larger and more powerful than the weak, lonely self." Sarton believes that before we can be ready to "belong" to anything, we must first take time to nurture a strong sense of self in solitude. Margaret Mead's study of the Manus Islanders offers an interesting contrast. She reports that a child's development of a strong, autonomous self depends on the ways family and community members consider the child an integrated, connected part of the social structure in his or her early years.

Option One: Write an essay in which you clarify for yourself the ways your own sense of individuality has come into conflict with the needs or expectations of others. You might want to ask yourself some of the following questions (or come up with your own) to help give a focus to your writing: Do you seek solitude or go somewhere in particular when you feel the need to consider yourself as an individual? Have there been times when you have purposely gone against a rule or the status quo because you felt it was wrong or it dampened your style? Have there been times when what you wanted hasn't been what another person you care about wanted? Have there been times when you made yourself stand out in a crowd by the way you looked or acted? Do you hold beliefs that seem unique to you, that your friends and family members do not hold? Do you believe that you are special in some way that others do not acknowledge?

Option Two: Mark Twain wrote, "We are creatures of <u>out-side influences</u>—we originate <u>nothing</u> within. Whenever we take a new line of thought and drift into a new line of belief and action, the impulse is <u>always</u> suggested from the <u>out-side</u>." To prepare for this assignment, jot down some of the special talents or abilities you have developed over the years. These might include (but are in no way limited to) a talent for art or music, a special ability in sports, a proclivity toward the love of nature, or perhaps simply the desire to spend time alone or to help others. Then, write an essay in which you clarify for yourself the ways other people or particular events in your life have helped to shape that special quality you possess.

ASSIGNMENT TWO

Readings: Virginia Woolf, from <u>A Room of One's Own</u>.

   Marc Feigen Fasteau, "Friendships Among Men."

"THE SELF AND OTHERS"

Virginia Woolf creates the imaginary Judith Shakespeare to demonstrate how women's subordinate status historically has prevented them from the kinds of creative achievements that men have accomplished. According to Woolf, this status relegated women to the role of helpmates, rather than independent persons in their own right. Marc Feigen Fasteau points out that gender stereotypes are deeply embedded in our social structure, and we have difficulty escaping their influence, even when it becomes apparent that they severely limit us. In the first assignment, you explored your own individuality. In this assignment, you will look at how stereotypes influence our determinations of ourselves and others.

Option One: Think about some of the programs that are currently on television. Do they do a good job of mirroring modern images of men and women? In your opinion, are those images positive or negative? Write an essay in which you inform your readers whether or not you believe television portrays authentic images of men and women. Be sure to include plenty of examples from a variety of programming. Be aware that before you can explain how gender stereotypes show up on television, you need to define how they manifest themselves in real life.

Option Two: Interview someone you know who you think has surpassed his or her traditional gender role—for instance, a woman who excels at a job that was once considered strictly a man's domain, or a man who has overcome the masculine stereotype that Fasteau describes. Write an essay in which you inform your readers about what you think is the secret of that person's success. What specific cultural biases did this person have to overcome? What personal qualities enabled him or her to overcome them? Before your interview, either on your own or with classmates, compile a good list of questions to ask during the interview. Keep in mind that you may want to quote directly or paraphrase some of the things the person says in the interview, so bring a tape recorder or a sturdy pad for taking notes.

ASSIGNMENT THREE

Readings: Pope John Paul II, "On Human Work."

Huston Smith, "The Hindu Way to God through Work."

Barbara Ehrenreich, "Farewell to Work."

"THE SELF AND WORK"

Christianity and Hinduism offer two very different reasons for working, but both declare that work, or activity, is a natural drive in humans. Ehrenreich argues that work is simply part of an economic power struggle—it's not "natural" at all. As you prepare for this assignment, consider some of the consequences of each of these philosophies. We spend a great deal of time at work, and the type of work we choose often defines us for others. So far in this sequence, you have considered your individuality and investigated how stereotypes affect you. In this assignment, think about how your attitudes toward work affect who you are.

Option One: Write an essay explaining what has made you want to become educated for a particular career. Even if you haven't yet chosen a career, do you feel the need to do so? Why or why not? In your essay, demonstrate the importance—or unimportance—of choosing the "right" career. You may want to think about some of these questions as you prepare to write: What are the factors you consider when thinking about a career? Which of these factors are most important? Why? Is this level of importance dictated by you or someone else? Would you like the process of choosing a career to be different? If so, how and why?

Option Two: Write an essay in which you first explain America's work ethic. Is the typical American worker hungry for power? Does he or she simply have an urge to be active? Is he or she driven by an urge to make the world a better place? Are there other explanations for the work ethic? Then evaluate the work ethic. Should it be different or the same? Why? You may want to consider some of these questions: What should be of the utmost importance where work is concerned, the good of the individual or the good of the community? Why? Should they be of equal importance? Can such a division even be drawn? How would your vision of an ideal

work ethic play itself out in real-world terms, in real consequences?

ASSIGNMENT FOUR

Readings: Plato, "Crito."

Martin Luther King, Jr., "Letter from Birmingham
Jail."

"THE SELF AND GOVERNMENT"

While some governments give special groups preferential
treatment, others try to determine what is best for all groups.
Either of these practices can create conflict for any particular
individual. As you work on this assignment, keep in mind what
you have determined about the way a person's sense of self
is influenced by stereotypes and by work. For this assignment, you will explore the areas where the self and government come into contact.

Option One: Socrates and Martin Luther King, Jr., both try
to change the way people think. Socrates uses his skills as a
teacher and philosopher to encourage critical thinking in Plato
and the Athenian youth. King uses his talent as a writer and
minister to try to change the narrow-mindedness of bigotry
and the laws that allow it. But Socrates and King differ over
the role that government should play in our activities. How far
should the government be allowed to control what we do to
persuade others? Is there a distinction between physical and
verbal persuasion? If a statement or work of art has the
potential to harm certain people or incite dangerous behavior,
should censorship be allowed? Write a letter about censorship
to a newspaper of your choice. Try to persuade its readers
that the government should or should not be allowed to cen-
sor, and under what conditions. Use examples from both the
readings for this assignment and from your own ideas and
experiences.

Option Two: Both Socrates and Martin Luther King, Jr.,
were jailed for doing something they thought right. Socrates
argues that, even though he thinks his sentence is wrong, to
be a good citizen he must accept it. King, on the other hand,
feels that, as an upright person, he cannot accept what he
views as the injustice of his sentence. Thus, the two men
disagree about who determines the standards of justice. Does
the government know what is best for us, or does the individual? Write an essay in which you try to persuade your classmates that either the government or the individual should decide what justice is and who should be served by it. Use
examples from both essays to support your ideas.

ISSUES FOR DISCUSSION

• What do you think of the subject Don selected for this sequence?
Do you agree that "the self" is a subject that all college students are

inherently interested in? What are some potential problems in requiring students to write about this subject?

• About three weeks into the term, one of Don's students came to his office for help on a draft. After Don read through the piece carefully and worked very hard suggesting possible ways to explore and develop the ideas more fully, the student sighed in frustration, "Gosh, I didn't know I was signing up for a philosophy class. I thought this was just composition." How should Don respond to this student's concern?

• In the week following midterm break, Don was a few minutes late for class, and several members began to discuss, in a rather heated fashion, how tired they were of thinking and writing about the self. By the time Don got to the room, the students had elected a spokesperson to ask him, "Is there any chance we could write about something else besides the self? There are lots of other interesting things in the readings. Why can't we write about whatever we feel like?" How should Don respond to these questions?

• Don believes that students should be exposed to a variety of prose genres—that they should see each genre as representing "a certain community's ways of responding to intellectual questions." But when his writing assignments refer to the readings, they ignore the "certain communities" to which the readings were addressed. Is it appropriate to treat readings about a subject such as "the self" as if where they were written did not matter? In what community will the students perceive themselves to be participating as they write for Don's class?

• Don had hoped that his sequence would encourage the students to see their essays as "spiraling" one into the next, yet he found that only a few students were actually using ideas and material they had developed in previous essays in the succeeding ones. Most of his students were still treating each assignment as an isolated entity. What can Don do to encourage the students to see the course as a unified intellectual endeavor? Are the assignments sufficiently explicit on how writing each one is relevant to writing the next?

• Don wanted his sequence of assignments to elicit writing that accomplished a range of purposes. He had thought about labeling assignments explicitly as "self-expressive," "informative," "exploratory," "demonstrative," and "persuasive," but he decided against it, thinking that these terms too much resembled "teacher-talk" that would seem foreign to students. What do you think of Don's decision? Would such labels on the assignments have helped his students understand what primary type of writing the assignment was designed to elicit? Would such labels suggest that the *real* purpose of responding to the assignment sequence was to practice writing for different purposes, rather than to pursue inquiry of a subject?

• Don declares in his memo that what students transfer from a writing course is an understanding that writing is a way of learning about a subject, together with some ability to use writing to learn. What do you think his students will learn about "the self" by taking Don's course?

• Would Don's students learn more about their subject if they engaged the readings more closely? if the readings were different? if the reasons for inquiry about "the self" were more specifically defined?

• For the final paper of the sequence, the one with the options concerning censorship and justice, one student came to Don with a special request. She had developed a strong interest in the issue of an individual's right to privacy, and she had been doing considerable reading on that subject. Because, she reasoned, this issue was pretty close to the ones Don listed in assignment four, she wondered if she could write her final paper on that subject. How should Don respond?

• How do you think assignment three, option two, on America's work ethic would compare with an assignment that students might be given on the same general subject in a sociology course? a history course? How would expectations for support and claims for support be different?

• Don values originality in his students' writing. He believes that students rarely get a chance to be original, and composition classes should give them that opportunity. Is he right? How can the value of originality and the value of learning be taken into account?

A Political Critique Course

Sona Patel is herself deeply involved in cultural studies, and she believes that her students should come to understand writing as collective praxis. To help them recognize the presence of ideology in all discourse, she will assign some sophisticated readings on post-Saussurean linguistics. Her students will also read cultural critiques by a number of writers— dramatic, complex expressions of resistance to culturally produced "truths" about gender, race, and class.

Sona will focus on writers' positions and goals, and she will encourage her students to see their own writing as action that has consequences. The students will often be asked to write during class, and more formal writing will be assigned in conjunction with readings that define the three segments of the course. During the first segments there will be short papers; during the second segment the students will keep a journal and submit "a critical report" based on their journal entries; during the final segment a paper will be required—a paper treating the central concept of the course and "acting on" the last set of readings. In addition, Sona invites guest speakers from the Marginal Pedagogy Group, whose members are her teaching colleagues.

Sona's course, which she titles "(Re)Writing Culture," is attracting a lot of attention among her colleagues: as one version of freshman composition, it appears to present attractive opportunities and serious hazards at the same time.

Freshman Composition Syllabus

Ah, what an age it is
When to speak of trees is almost a crime
For it is a kind of silence about injustice!

The point, of course, is not whether we speak of trees but the uses of our doing so. In other words, let's ask how—rather why—we speak about anything. This course examines the effectiveness of a range of practices in culture: the classroom shall be a space for (re)writing texts of culture: an ad, an essay, a glance, a gaze, noise, a strike, a slogan, the auctioneer's shout, a film, an interview, a politician's face, the classroom . . . Our investigations will be divided into three interrelated sections: (a) Writing in Culture, (b) Culture as Writing, and (c) Writing as Collective Praxis. Throughout the course, our attempt will be to understand writing (and a class on composition and communication) in terms of culture, representation, history, the subject, ideology, and critique.

The texts mentioned below have been duplicated and are available at the campus copy center. You are advised to consult the texts placed on reserve under the instructor's name for additional readings or for research on specific topics of interest.

(a) Writing in Culture

In my time streets led to the quicksand.
Speech betrayed me to the slaughterer.
There was little I could do. But without me
The rulers would have been more secure. This was my hope.

This part of the course will be used to raise fundamental questions about the relation of writing to culture. Our collective attempt will be to move beyond the trivialities of concerns that limit attention to the mechanics of writing. The class shall examine the (in)adequacy of questions like "Do you feel comfortable using a computer or would you prefer a pen?" The class shall begin to develop a theory of writing by asking specific questions about the uses and modes of intelligibility adopted by readers/writers occupying different positions in culture. We might ask: "What allows Orwell to say that the best writing is that in which the self has been effaced? And what is at stake for Rich when she asserts that she must write as a woman?" Similarly, our attention to textuality will allow us to raise questions not, as is fashionable, about the play of signifiers, but about the various ways in which culture inscribes meaning as modalities of textuality: meaning through differences, discriminations, and hierarchy.

The Question of Materiality (Jan. 3-13):

Barbara Harlow, "Prison Memoirs of Political Detainees"
Malcolm X, "Coming to an Awareness of Language"
Mel Gussow, "From the City Streets, a Poet of the Stage"
John Berger, "Ways of Seeing"

The Question of Subjectivity (Jan.16-25):

George Orwell, "Why Do I Write?"
Bertolt Brecht, "The Worker Reads History"
Pablo Neruda, "United Fruit Co."
Adrienne Rich, "When We Dead Re-Awaken: Writing as Re-Vision"

The Question of Textuality (Jan. 27-Feb. 3):

Robin Lakoff, "You Are What You Say"
Tomas Guillen, "What to Call an American of Hispanic Descent"
Consumers Union, "It's Natural! It's Organic! Or Is It?"
Nicolas Guillen, "Problems of Underdevelopment"

(b) Culture as Writing

This part of the course will be organized around a series of lecture-workshops to be led by teachers of writing who will be able to bring to our classroom an extensive range of interests and urgencies. Culture will be examined as a site (or a "text") where both dominant and oppositional ideologies inscribe their "truths." The classroom will function as a transdisciplinary space where discourses from philosophy to film studies, psychoanalysis to journalism, and music to political science can intersect and inform our interrogation of the ways of "making sense" in our culture. The effort, on our part, will not be simply to gain access to a "variety" of discourses but, instead, to see how the "real" is produced in culture in so many complex and interrelated ways. Students will continue to do in-class writing but, instead of writing short papers, the students will be expected to maintain a journal. At the end of this section, on March 1, each student will present a critical report based upon journal entries.

1. "Discourses of Seeing: City Space, Slums, Walls, and Graffiti." Guest Speaker 1. (Feb. 6) Read Catherine Belsey's "Criticism and Meaning."
2. "Citibank Visa Ad: What Gets You Credit on Television?"

Guest Speaker 2. (Feb. 8) Read Ellen Seiter's "Semiotics and Television."

3. "Discourses of Hearing: Popular Music and Representation of Race." Guest Speaker 3. (Feb. 10) Read "James Taylor Marked for Death," by Lester Bangs.

4. "The Classroom as a Political Site." Colloquia with Members of the Marginal Pedagogy Group. (Feb. 13 and Feb. 15)

5. "Mass Culture and the Eclipse of Reason." Guest Speaker 4. (Feb. 17) Read handout.

6. "Discourses of Sexuality: Feminism and the Politics of the Gaze." Guest Speaker 5. (Feb. 21) Read "Take Me, Hurt Me, Smoke Me," by John Leo.

7. "The Worker, Strikes, and the Media." Guest Speaker 6. (Feb. 24) Read Roland Barthes's "The Men in the Street on Strike."

(c) Writing as Collective Praxis

On a Chinese Carving of a Lion:

The bad fear your claws.
The good enjoy your elegance.
This
I would like to hear said
Of my verse.

Bell Hooks, "Coming to Voice" (March 3)

Aime Cesaire, "Discourse on Colonialism" (March 7)

Terry Eagleton, "The Author as Producer"

Conventional textbooks of composition suggest formal techniques like brainstorming, freewriting, clustering, etc. as means of overcoming writer's block. Hooks, on the other hand, directs us not to the "how" but to the "why" of the problem:

"Encouraging students to speak, I tell them to imagine what it must mean to live in a culture where to speak one risks imprisonment, torture, and death. I ask them to think about what it means that they lack the courage to speak in a situation where there are few if any consequences. Can their fear be understood solely as an expression of shyness? Or is it an expression of deeply embedded, socially constructed restrictions against speech in a culture of domination, fear of owning one's words, or taking a stand?"

To write, then, is to produce consequences. Aime Cesaire's text is exemplary in the sense that it examines the consequences of one type of writing (the writing of the "apologists" of colonialism) and sets up in opposition to that type of writing the anticolonialist discourse which has radically different, liberatory consequences. In other words, Cesaire's text shows the effectivity of writing as critique. The class will study Cesaire's text not merely as exemplifying clear paragraph divi-

sion and appropriate choice of words, but, by asking the
question "for what?" the class will relate these rhetorical devices to their ends. To put it differently, Cesaire's text helps us
move beyond the fetishization of punctuation to the more important task of foregrounding the goals of any piece of writing.

Finally, the class will discuss Terry Eagleton's "The Author
as Producer." The conventional approach to composition (and
by "conventional" I do not mean "traditional" or "old" so
much as the "dominant" and the "commonsensical"—being
up-to-date is not an advance in itself) relies on such cliches
as "process" and "revision." Eagleton's text helps us prob-
lematize these acts by suggesting that what needs to be
changed is not simply the view that writing is a practice instead of a product but, more importantly, it is the romantic
notion of the author as creator which has to be replaced by
the historical idea of the author as producer. The individualist,
inspirational figure thereby gives way to the worker acting in a
social context. With this, the concept of "group revision" gets
transformed from an exercise in "sharing" to an engagement
with what Eagleton (following Brecht and Benjamin) describes
as ". . . how far the artist reconstructs the artistic forms at his
disposal, turning authors, readers and spectators into collabo-
rators."

The final paper will be on a topic of the student's choice. The
formulation of the topic as well as the paper's writing and
evaluation will be done by the students in workshops that will
be held March 3-13. The final paper will not be expected to
so much reflect as to act on the final three readings; in a
sense, therefore, the final paper will take a position with regards to the idea of writing as collective praxis. (By "praxis"
we can understand the process of forming, grasping, and
changing oneself and a world—necessarily historical—through
productive activities.)

Attendance is required. There will be no conventional examinations. Grades will be determined by evaluating the student's participation in class and workshops (40%) and the
three papers (60%). Grading follows the policy outlined in the
college bulletin: C indicates work which meets the course requirements in every way, and is the normal grade. B and A
are grades given for work which shows standards of excel-
lence, with A indicating outstanding achievement. University
policy on conduct applies.

ISSUES FOR DISCUSSION

• Will this course turn out to be an intellectually exciting experience?
Examining readers' and writers' positions and practices in their own
culture will be a new, potentially stimulating activity for students. Also,

Sona Patel's own investment is clear, and she wants her students to be mutual participants in inquiry. But the first hazard would seem to be accessibility of key ideas.

The syllabus immediately confronts the students with unfamiliar concepts and ways of speaking. What, for example, will the students make of this statement: "Our attention to textuality will allow us to raise questions . . . about the various ways in which culture inscribes meaning as modalities of textuality: meaning through difference, discrimination, and hierarchy"? Could the syllabus be rewritten so that it is more readily understandable? Would such rewriting constitute mystification or the service of inappropriate values? New terms are going to appear in the course readings in any case. Is it just as well that such terms appear immediately and in the ways they do?

Course readings often assume reference points that students will not have, and, as critiques of cultural practices, the readings will challenge much that has been implicit in the students' earlier learning. Will so many new assumptions, new targets, and new goals leave students bewildered? If it is important that they fully understand each piece, should the number of readings be reduced? If full understanding is not expected, will the students merely learn to use, earnestly or cynically, a new set of clichés?

• The one thing likely to be clear when her students first read the syllabus is that Sona will take a strong, explicitly political stance. Will most of the students be intrigued by new radical arguments, or will large numbers drop the course after the first day? Sona may assume that some students will disappear, but she may consider that unavoidable. Would you agree?

• Readings for the course include various kinds of texts, but ideologically they all move in the same direction. Would it be a good idea to include some texts explicitly representing opposed views and to ask the students to articulate their response? They might, for example, be given the following lines from Dinesh D'Souza's "Illiberal Education": "One can discover in the new scholarship a justification for the systematic venting of grievances against the basic systems of American society, which the new scholars commonly consider 'institutionally racist.' These systems—democracy, the free market, due process, and so on—are largely procedural, and are intended to establish a neutral framework that allows all citizens to pursue happiness and safeguard their rights."

• Would exploring the assertion that our "largely procedural" cultural systems establish a "neutral framework" sensitize skeptical students, making them more receptive to the assigned cultural critiques? Or would the presence of opposite, published views tend to enhance the perceived legitimacy of those views, perhaps increasing polarization in the class?

• In the middle of the course, the class has its first of two sessions with a member of the Marginal Pedagogy Group as guest speaker. Sona planned this class session as an opportunity to discuss "the classroom as a political site." Students are all too rarely invited to analyze their own courses and classrooms, and she hopes these sessions will encourage serious, open discussion of ideas about teaching, learning, and the nature of knowledge.

During the class session, a highly charged political atmosphere prevails.

About fifteen minutes into the class, one student interrupts angrily, questioning the critical implications of the readings, even resisting the fundamental ideas that underlie the syllabus as whole. What do you think the student might say? How do you think Sona should react?

In the ensuing discussion, a student announces her unequivocal support of the Marginal Pedagogy Group's agenda. What do you think she might say? How should Sona and the guest speaker respond?

• Topics for the students' final papers are to be formulated in workshops, and the workshop groups will also evaluate the papers once they are complete. For the students to assume such mutual responsibilities is appropriate as the climax to Sona's course. And, ideally, the workshops will foster what educational philosopher Ewa Pytowska has called the true meaning of the word "individuality," which each person experiences when tied to others by a common goal and the boundaries of a common path. However, success in the workshops will require mutual understanding of the goal and the path, that is, of the purpose of the final papers and the boundaries of the acceptable approach. Descriptions of the final paper assignment in the syllabus are quite general and abstract. Can you envision possible topics? Could you devise activities that would help the students to formulate topics and judge their promise?

• What about evaluating the papers once they are written? Should the students have read or discussed each other's writing earlier in the course? Will ideological differences place a special strain on evaluation? What criteria should the students employ? Should Sona provide criteria, or should the students develop them?

• In her syllabus, Sona characterizes "conventional" writing instruction scornfully: her class will "move beyond the trivialities of concerns that limit attention to the *mechanics* of writing ... [and] examine the (in)adequacy of questions like 'Do you feel comfortable using a computer or would you prefer a pen?'" The class will study a theoretical text "not merely as exemplifying clear paragraph division and appropriate choice of words, but by asking the question 'for what?' the class will relate these rhetorical devices to their ends." Her class will "move beyond the fetishization of punctuation to the more important task of foregrounding the goals of any piece of writing." She will focus not on "formal techniques like brainstorming, freewriting, clustering" to overcome writer's block, but on reasons why writer's block occurs. Similarly, she will not rely on "such clichés as 'process' and 'revision.'" Instead, her class readings will help the students see writers as *producers* in social situations, not as isolated, inspired (or uninspired) *creators*.

Is her negative characterization of "conventional" writing instruction justified? What do you consider the most important elements in it? How are her criticisms related to cultural critique as her course theme? Can her criticisms be taken into account by other teachers in other ways?

• In what sense will Sona's own course teach writing? When addressing her students as readers, Sona urges them to focus on published writers' goals, on their reasons for saying things. Does the syllabus suggest that she will give adequate, parallel attention to goals when she asks her students to write? Her writing assignments are unspecified: what topics would be appropriate for the short papers and journal entries she speaks of? What uses might she make of students' writing in her course?

A Linked Writing Course

Cesar Soliz knows that when expository writing is evaluated, substance—what is said—is almost always considered most important. He also knows that substance in his own writing comes mainly from grappling with ideas and problems relevant to the people for whom, and among whom, he writes. He has taught general composition courses and tried hard to help his students grapple with their topics, for he wants them to realize that writing is not only a way of recording and communicating thoughts, but a way of developing and critiquing thoughts—in effect, a way of generating new understanding for the writer.

But his efforts to teach writing as engagement in inquiry have not been particularly successful. Cesar thinks he knows at least some of the reasons: he has provided readings as a basis for writing assignments, readings all related to a theme, but as resources those readings have been limited. More important, his students have not had reason to *study* the readings except insofar as this was necessary to produce assigned writing. The students were, after all, taking a writing course, and they saw themselves as practicing, doing exercises so that they would be prepared for *real* writing occasions elsewhere. The topics they read and wrote about seemed simply arbitrary choices made by the instructor.

To take advantage of his students' own academic interests and resources and their reasons for writing, Cesar has encouraged them to work on a writing assignment for another course they are taking in lieu of one of his own assignments. The students are generally grateful for this opportunity, but results are mixed. Incorporating assignments for other courses naturally disrupts Cesar's assignment sequence, and the "incorporation" itself is often weak. Students with writing assignments in other courses are taking *different* courses in *different* disciplines, so they do not know each other's contexts and Cesar does not know their contexts either. As a result, comments on the students' drafts tend to be on matters of form only. When comments on substance are made, the student writers sometimes reject them as inappropriate to their purpose. This happens when the students' understanding of their own writing contexts is sufficiently clear. When it isn't, the students may accept Cesar's comments on substance, then suffer when their readers in another course criticize their work.

Cesar discusses his frustration with a friend who teaches at another university in a program that links writing courses with general education lecture courses in various disciplines. His friend says linked writing courses take some time to get used to, but they offer great opportunities to teach writing as engagement in inquiry.

Cesar decides to consider an experiment. He gets some advice from his friend, then makes an appointment to discuss possibilities with a faculty member in the sociology department. He chooses sociology because he took a few courses in the field when he was an undergraduate, and because the sociology department at his school offers well-regarded lecture courses taken by large numbers of freshmen and sophomores. He chooses a particular faculty member because she has a reputation as an excellent teacher, and she is interested in the problem of general education.

In their initial talk, Cesar makes it clear that he is thinking about a link arrangement where the writing course and the lecture course will carry equal amounts of credit and be graded separately. But the two courses will be closely related and mutually supportive: materials and purposes for writing in the writing course will be drawn from the lecture course, and there will probably be at least one joint paper assignment. Cesar will be able to exploit the lecture courses as an interpretive community in which his writing students are learning to participate. The sociology teacher is enthusiastic because students who take both courses will almost inevitably learn more of what she is most interested in teaching, and, in some sense, they will learn better—*using* new information, evaluating ideas, learning to think critically.

Cesar wants to pursue the experiment, and he knows he will need to write a formal proposal to be considered by a curriculum committee. But before preparing the proposal, he decides to visit his friend's campus, sit in on some linked writing classes, talk to teachers, and collect sample syllabi and assignments. He visits three classes, each linked with a lecture in a different discipline; he finds that, within their common design, special problems and opportunities distinguish each class. He spends the most time studying the writing course linked with a sociology lecture course called "Theories of Crime." The calendar that follows includes (1) the lecture and reading topics for the sociology course and (2) the discussion topics, activities, and assignments for the writing link course.

SOCIOLOGY, Week 1

Definitions of crime
Nature and role of theories: generating hypotheses
Testing hypotheses: sociology's focus on methods
Four major methods, and limitations of each. A researcher might use:
1. Official records (U.S. Census, Uniform Crime Reports)
2. Victimization surveys (National Crime Survey)
3. Self-reports (local surveys of particular groups)
4. Case studies

WRITING LINK, Week 1

Opening class discussion
—What makes writing "good"?
—What kinds of comments on papers in the past have been helpful? useless?
—Writers' contexts and purposes as the key to commenting

First overnight assignment:
Study a paper assignment and a sample draft from this Sociology Writing Link last year (distributed). Write comments on the draft.

Second class meeting:
Class examines another copy of the draft from last year,

this one bearing the comments of a student in last year's class. Class members compare their comments with those of last year's student and discuss the differences. They examine the revised paper in relation to comments on the draft.

Second overnight assignment:

Begin thinking about what kind of crime you will concentrate on in researching and writing this term. Also, prepare to discuss questions you have about theory, raised by opening sociology lectures.

Third class meeting:

Class examines the Wallace Wheel, a graphic representation of what a hypothesis is and how it relates to theory. Discussion of evidence and method issues in sociology.

Third overnight assignment:

In 1-3 pages, explain your theory of crime (or one kind of crime, if you prefer). Remember, the sociology lecturer said yesterday that a theory must define crime, argue the causes of crime, and suggest solutions to crime. Be sure your theory includes these three elements. Bring a total of 4 copies to class.

Fourth class meeting:

In groups of three, students read each other's theory statements. Each writes at least one question in response to each statement read in the group, and groups discuss strengths and weaknesses they see. One copy of each theory statement, together with questions, is turned in. <u>Students save their own copy</u> of these early statements for use later.

SOCIOLOGY, Week 2

Types or theories of crime

Micro vs. macro levels of analysis

Conflict vs. consensus types of explanations

WRITING LINK, Week 2

To practice critical reading, students examine an article from a sociology journal published in the '80s—a very poor article (referred to in lecture) on capital punishment as a deterrent. Overnight, students write short summaries of the argument, then list 3-5 problems they see (or questions they have) and 3-5 positive features—reasons the article, despite problems, may be worth reading.

Problems are identified by asking key questions given in Week 1 sociology lectures on methodology. In class, students meet in small groups to compare argument summaries, then strengths and weaknesses they've identified. Finally, the full class evaluates the article in open discussion.

Next, the class meets in the library for an introduction to 3-4 major journals in sociology and criminology. Work begins toward Paper assignment 1: First, choose the kind of crime you will study. Some possible choices: Rape (stranger or acquaintance), child abuse (physical or sexual), homicide, juvenile delinquency, police violence, hate crimes (gay bashing, racially motivated crimes), burglary, assault, spouse abuse (wife-battering), white collar or elite crime, political crime, environmental crime, drug-related crime (abuse, sales, production), prostitution.

In the journal literature, find two arguments that make causal arguments about the specific crime or kind of criminal behavior you have chosen. Try to find articles that disagree about cause. (Although disagreement is not a requirement, it may make your task easier here.) Study the articles carefully. Then write a paper arguing that one article is more convincing than the other, using standards presented in the sociology course to make your evaluation. 5-6 pages.

SOCIOLOGY, Week 3

Specific theories of crime and studies that test them:

Classical School

Positivism

Social Darwinism

In moving through this sequence, the lecturer identifies theories in their historical and professional contexts, describes key features of theories, and discusses studies relevant to them.

WRITING LINK, Week 3

Small-group discussion:

Groups are arranged by topic-related groups of crime. Groups share resources and research tips. Then they critique tentative thesis statements for Paper 1.

Full class discussion

Sample student response to Paper 1 assignment from previous year: students' and teacher's critical evaluation with text on overhead.

Short conferences

Each student meets with the writing link teacher to discuss problems, plans, tentative opening for Paper 1.

SOCIOLOGY, Week 4

Structural Functionalism

Strain/"Anomie" Theories

The lecturer regularly asks challenging questions, such as how a given theory could be tested or whether a given study supports, refutes, or challenges a theory. Also, at the end of almost every class meeting, she requires the students to write a one-minute paper; these are usually brief summaries followed by a reaction or a question. She reads several aloud to begin the next class meeting and makes several comments. Other required writing: essays on exams and a paper due in Week 10, jointly assigned in the writing link.

WRITING LINK, Week 4

Due: Draft of Paper 1, 4 copies

Reading groups exchange drafts, and a copy of each draft goes to the writing link teacher.
Overnight, students comment in writing, then discuss drafts.
Students have half-hour conferences with the writing link teacher, focusing on drafts, reading group responses, and revision plans.

Due last day of Week 4: Final version of Paper 1, turned in with commented drafts.

SOCIOLOGY, Week 5

Review

Midterm examination

Social Disorganization Theory: Chicago School

WRITING LINK, Week 5

Discussion: Paper 1—three students' essays copied for discussion of sociological issues raised and rhetorical strategies employed.

Further library work begun to prepare for Paper assignment 2:

Critically review more of the literature on the crime you are studying, then formulate and argue for your own hypothesis about its cause. You must make use of articles from sociological journals, but you may also use other kinds of research, such as self-report surveys, case studies, or interviews. In presenting your argument, explain at least one opposing view, and carefully refute it. 6-8 pages.

SOCIOLOGY, Week 6

Differential Association Theory

Neutralization Theory

WRITING LINK, Week 6

Discussion: Research problems and methodology questions raised by Paper 2—especially on the use of different kinds of evidence.

Small groups: Exchange and discuss hypotheses and current research questions.

Short conferences

Due: Tentative openings for Paper 2, with copies for discussing in reading groups.

SOCIOLOGY, Week 7

Control—Social Bonding Theories

WRITING LINK, Week 7

Due: Draft of Paper 2, with copies for reading groups and the
writing link teacher. Students write comments, then meet to
discuss drafts.
Half-hour individual conferences with the writing link
teacher. (Class does not meet during the conference period.)
Due last day of Week 7: Final version of Paper 2, turned in
with commented draft.

SOCIOLOGY, Week 8

Labeling Theory
Conflict Theories

WRITING LINK, Week 8

Class discussion and out-of-class assignment: To clarify and
organize the many theories presented in the sociology
course—and to prepare for writing Paper 3, students make
theory charts.

First, in class, all the theories anybody can think of are
listed on the board. Then the list is refined by tossing out
theories no longer of interest and by figuring out relations
among theories, e.g., whether a given item is a theory in itself
or part of a larger theory. Discrepancies between lecture presentation and textbook presentation of theories are discussed.

All students will make their own charts, so individuals' lists
vary. Each must decide, however, how to arrange the theories
chosen—chronologically? micro/macro? consensus/conflict?
Even more important, what will go on the other axis—on what
bases will theories be compared? Students must include four
key categories, but they generate the rest of the terms of
analysis on their own. Drafts of charts are discusssed in
groups, and revised charts are turned in with the draft of
Paper 3.

SOCIOLOGY, Week 9

Conflict Theories (continued)

WRITING LINK, Week 9

Paper assignment 3: "Evaluate three theories of crime, arguing for the one you think best explains its cause and presenting the policy implications of your choice.

One of the three theories you use must be the one you
wrote about during the first week of class. Your theory charts

should help you select the other two theories, and suggest possible arguments. You need to refute the two theories you reject, as well as support the one you think is best. Also, your policy discussion must be logically consistent with the theory you select. Your argument should include:

—A brief summary of your earlier ideas on the causes of crime
—Evidence and reasoning that support your selection of one theory and rejection of two others
—Discussion that shows you understand the persistent problems in the theory you have chosen, even though you think it provides the best explanation of crime
—Discussion of the policy implications (money-spending priorities) of your argument that are consistent with the theory you have selected as best ("If theory X is right about causes of crime, then in order to control crime, we need to. . . .") 5-6 pages.

SOCIOLOGY, Week 10

Review

Due last day of Week 10: Paper evaluating three theories of crime—paper also assigned in writing link

WRITING LINK, Week 10

Drafting, reading group consultations, revised theory charts submitted
Due last day of Week 10: Paper 3, with commented drafts

SOCIOLOGY, Week 11

Final examination

WRITING LINK, Week 11

Final conference on accumulated term's work

ISSUES FOR DISCUSSION

• Cesar's friend says that the paper assignments in his writing link are somewhat intimidating—certainly more specific and complex than paper assignments he used to give in general composition classes. Yet the students write more and seem to assume more responsibility for their writing in his linked course than they did in general composition. Why might that be?

• While Cesar's friend is pleased that his writing link students show more commitment and are more assertive about what they need to learn, he at first found this rather disconcerting, even threatening to his own authority. His authority seemed threatened, too, by the fact that discussion in his class often focused on theories, cases, and questions relevant to the sociology course, but he was not a sociologist. The director of his program suggested that, on occasions like this, he think of himself as a Master Learner. What would a Master Learner's role be? How might it be played in a writing link class?

• Cesar wants to follow his friend's practice, studying and utilizing a sociology lecture class as "an interpretive community in which writing students are learning to participate." He intends to take seriously the purposes of sociology as he designs writing assignments and responds to students' work. But he is worried about jargon issues. Should he accept specialized language as community-defining? Would that mean approving all language in, say, sociology journal articles? How will the students' writing be affected by efforts to use specialized language? Should the students' use of such language be discouraged?

• Cesar's friend says that his grades on the final, jointly assigned papers are usually the same as or very close to the sociologist's grades—but occasionally there is a discrepancy. Since the writing link course and the lecture course are graded separately, this is not technically a problem, but the students are likely to raise questions. Should the writing link teacher offer to reread papers he has graded, without promising any grade change? Should he examine both graded copies, again without promising any change? Should he discuss grade discrepancies with the sociologist? Should he simply tell the students that different readers read differently, and encourage the students to decide for themselves which reading is more appropriate or more helpful? Should he explain that the two courses have different agendas, even though the writing course deliberately focuses on sociologists' writing purposes? How could he explain the difference?

• In order to become familiar with the writing demands and evaluation issues likely to arise in the sociology context, Cesar plans to borrow from the sociologist on his campus some copies of student papers from the past. What else could Cesar do in advance or during the term to improve his own perspective as a reader? What other measures could he take to minimize any grading discrepancies?

• Many recent textbooks for composition classes emphasize readings as models, as sources of information, and as context-definers for research and writing. Among the textbooks organized by general academic fields or disciplines are *The Researching Reader: Source-Based Writings across the Disciplines,* by Diane Dowdey, and *Writing in the Disciplines: A Reader for Writers,* by Mary Lynch Kennedy, William J. Kennedy, and Hadley M. Smith. The middle section of *The Researching Reader* is on the social sciences. It includes an orientation to social science research and one or two articles to represent each of six social science disciplines. Sociology is represented by an excerpt from *Middletown,* a study of Muncie, Indiana, published in 1929 (quoted in Kennedy, Kennedy, and Smith); and an excerpt from *An American Dilemma,* a study of race relations published in 1944 (quoted in Kennedy, Kennedy, and Smith). At the end of the middle section, the text offers several "writing assignments in the social sciences," including the two that follow:

> Research the impact of *The American Dilemma* on American policies. Examine the changes in the living conditions of blacks from 1940 to 1980. Compare the legal and economic condition. Look at the changes since 1980. (Dowdey 1990, 378)

> Beulah MacDonald recently won a judgment against the United Ku Klux Klans of America for inciting the lynching of her son in Mobile, Alabama, in 1981. Research this case and other recent cases of lynching and racial violence in America. Try to determine the causes and the effects. (Dowdey 1990, 379)

How would you compare these writing assignments with the assignments given in the course Cesar visited, the writing link with the sociology department's "Theories of Crime"? How would you compare the contexts in which the assignments are addressed? How would you compare what the students are likely to learn?

• The other book, *Writing in the Disciplines,* has three thematically organized sections under "The Social Sciences." The first is on the family, the second is on poverty, and the third is called "Violence and Crime." The readings for that section are as follows:

VIOLENCE AND CRIME

M. L. Gilula and D. N. Daniels, "Violence and Man's Struggle to Adapt" (Gilula and Daniels are psychiatrists)

William Safire, "Vigilante" (Safire is a columnist)

William E. Burrows, "The American Vigilante" (Burrows is a professor of journalism)

Ellen Goodman, "The Fascination of the Goetz Case" (Goodman is a columnist)

Manning Marable, "The Subway Vigilante" (Marable is a columnist; he is also a professor of political science and sociology)

Albert Scardino, "After a Burglary" (Scardino is an editor for The New York Times)

Lance Morrow, "It's Time to Ban Handguns" (Morrow is an editor for Time magazine)

Jerry Farber, "Nonviolence for the Nonsaint" (Farber is an English professor)

At the end of the social sciences chapter, "synthesis assignments" are offered. The first three are as follows:

> Social scientists usually begin their studies by asking a question. They supply a tentative answer to the question in the form of a hypothesis or supposition. Then they try to verify their hypothesis with supporting evidence. Select three articles, one from each chapter in this unit, and write a paper in which you explain how each author (a) asks a preliminary question, (b) formulates a hypothesis, and (c) verifies the hypothesis with supporting evidence.
>
> Consider as a whole the various authors' views on the role of nature or biology versus the role of society and culture in shaping and conditioning human behavior. Write a paper in which you state a position on the relative importance of "nature versus nurture" in determining sexual differences, economic disparity, and propensities towards violence and aggression.
>
> Social science writing takes many different forms, among them: *summaries* and *abstracts* of research, *book reviews, surveys of the literature* on the topic under consideration, *case studies, analyses* of causes and effects, *descriptions* of behaviors and customs, *definitions* of concepts and terms. Review the articles in this unit, and write a paper in which you describe for students who are unfamiliar with social science writing three different forms, giving examples of each. (Kennedy, Kennedy, and Smith 1987, 391)

Again, how would you compare these assignments with those given in the writing link? How would you compare contexts? likely learning?

• When Cesar visited his friend's campus, he sat in on a total of three writing link classes: the link discussed above with "Theories of Crime" in sociology; the link with "The Ancient World" in history; and the link with "Introduction to International Political Economy" in international studies.

Cesar found that the students in the history course were reading primary sources—Thucydides' *The Peloponnesian War* and Tacitus' *The Annals of Ancient Rome.* There were two joint paper assignments, one focusing on each of the primary texts; two additional paper assignments were made in the writing link only. The two joint assignments called for interpretation, and they were difficult for reasons that were in some respects opposites. Students had to figure out what Thucydides thought of the Athenians, because he never explicitly says; then they had to read "through" or "past" what the moralizing Tacitus thought of various emperors to get at what his text told them about Roman life.

How would the reading and writing requirements for this course compare with those in the sociology writing link? What kinds of overnight assignments and class activities would be appropriate for this writing link with history?

• Students in the link with "Introduction to International Political Economy" faced still another kind of reading-writing requirement. In the international studies course, they heard lectures on economic and political developments in the world system since 1945, and they read articles, mostly arguments from journals on how such developments should be understood. In addition to their common readings on modernization theory, dependency theory, and so forth, they read independently on the country of their choice all term. On the basis of this independent reading, they wrote two papers, which were jointly assigned in the writing link. They had to come up with their own topics, and the topics had to be in the form of causal questions. The assignment was as follows:

> On the basis of your reading, write two papers, one focusing on a political situation or event, the other on an economic situation or event. Look for a puzzling change or an anomalous situation—something you would not expect. Your essay should attempt to explain why (not how) something happened or something exists. Begin by building a reader's sense of your question as a real question. If your answer involves a relationship between your country and another country or countries in the world system, give special attention to that.
> 5-8 pages for each paper.

Questions that the students formulated ranged from "Why, despite Mexico's efforts to limit foreign investment, do foreigners continue to control much of Mexico's industry?" and "Given the great enthusiasm for Mitterand's reforms when he was elected, why did he have to retract the reforms within a year?" to "From 1967 to 1970 the Nigerian federal government was fighting a war—a war against its own wealthiest region. Why was Nigeria nevertheless able to maintain a healthy, growing economy?"

Again, how would the reading and writing requirements for this course compare with those in the sociology writing link? What kinds of overnight assignments and class activities would be appropriate for a writing link with international studies?

• The writing links that Cesar visited accompany lower-division, general education courses, and the links can be used to satisfy the university's composition requirement. Do you think this is appropriate? What kind of relation could students be encouraged to see between writing in one discipline and writing in another? between academic writing and other kinds of writing?

A Writing and Literature Course

Dan Howells's university offers several different freshman writing courses, any one of which can satisfy the composition requirement. Graduate students always begin by teaching the general "College Writing" course, in which only a little reading is assigned, none of it literary. Dan has been looking forward to teaching one of the other freshman courses, the one called "Writing about Literature," and now, in his second year, he is about to get his opportunity. He finds, however, that developing a course design is somewhat trickier than he expected.

Until recently, the "Writing about Literature" course used a very fat anthology of poems, stories, plays, and essays. Most teachers just went for coverage, assigning some readings from each genre and requiring four papers, one for each genre. But maintaining the identity of the course as a *writing* course was a recurrent problem. Absorbed in selecting from the great number and the different kinds of readings, teachers gave little attention to what might be fundamental to writing about literature. Also, teachers felt they had to do a fair amount of lecturing because they so frequently shifted times, places, writers, and genres—students had to be given some background if they were to be able to read.

The composition advisory committee worried that writing was being neglected, and, periodically at least, they were right to worry. Some teachers remarked that they felt guilty but happy while discussing literature, dutiful but bored when they focused on writing. They perceived literature and writing as separate, competing subjects in a schizophrenic course.

The committee's concern about the integration and identity of "Writing about Literature" led to some changes during the year before Dan was assigned to the course. The key problem seemed to be that, while teachers did assign papers, they thought of "teaching writing" as something that could go on only on the occasional, isolated days when they discussed essay organization or stylistic options or revision techniques. It was decided that teachers should ask students to write much more frequently as part of their preparation for class meetings and as an in-class activity. More use of writing to explore and respond to the literature would help integrate the course, and writing would be more compellingly taught by teaching it indirectly, for example by asking students to employ and analyze and evaluate writing with respect to immediate class purposes.

But what exactly should those purposes be? What questions should students be learning to ask about literary texts? Making more use of students' confusions and disagreements and discoveries would naturally provoke questions about the students themselves as readers, as well as questions about authors and texts. Dealing with the range of questions would mean looking at literature in its current class context and in its larger cultural contexts, not merely at self-contained "works." This prospect was attractive to some of the teachers, for it would allow their own studies in contemporary theory to play some role. However, ideas about textuality and the generation of readers' responses would have to be mainly enacted, not presented, in this introductory class. Furthermore, students would need time to read and react and think about the significance of their reactions—more time than a long list of readings would permit. Also, they would need readings that they could readily relate to each other so that understandings could build. As many scholars have suggested (for example, Robert Scholes), students need to become "culturally at home" in texts, but they cannot become "at home" if they are swept up in a fast-flowing stream of texts that are disparate.

The advisory committee concluded that (1) "Writing about Literature" should assign fewer texts in a more limited number of types; (2) authors' contexts and students' responses should be studied together with the texts; and (3) students should write and read each other's writing more or less constantly: writing should further the development of ideas before becoming the vehicle of presentation.

To initiate the change, the committee dropped the fat anthology, then debated ways of defining a much more limited, readily relatable set of readings. They knew that teachers' backgrounds and interests varied widely, so in order to preserve some choice, they decided to offer genres as options: teachers could choose a poetry anthology, a drama anthology, or a fiction anthology, the latter limited to works written since 1940. Teachers might bring in occasional pieces from outside their anthology and in a different genre if they wished (for example, some Raymond Carver poems when reading a Carver story), but questions relevant to writing about literature were to be raised primarily in terms of readings in the anthology selected.

Dan has decided to work with fiction, although he was a little concerned when he found that he had not read many of the stories included in the fiction text—*The Norton Anthology of Contemporary Fiction* (Cassill)—and some of the authors were unfamiliar to him. Also, the text provides no headnotes or other apparatus, just the stories themselves in alphabetical order by author and the dates of their original publication. Dan is glad the text does not give canned questions about the readings, but he is anxious to get started developing questions of his own.

He is not so concerned about questions on individual stories; once his course gets going, the students will help develop those. What he wants to sort out first are the big questions, the questions to which his course will be a response. He has decided to start by finding out which stories last year's teachers chose, how some of these teachers grouped the stories, and what they called their groupings. When he looks through the files, he finds the reading sequences for two fiction-based "Writing about Literature" classes, each of them a teacher's first experiment with the new version of the course. The reading sequences, one compiled by Larry Oakes and the other by Janet Missavage, for ten-week terms are as follows:

I "Writing about Literature"   Teacher: Larry Oakes

Course Readings:
1. Introduction

Katharine Brush	Birthday Party (not in anthology)
Alice Adams	Barcelona

2. Life as Story; Story as Life/Point of View

Woody Allen	The Kugelmass Episode
Gabriel Garcia Marquez	The Handsomest Drowned Man in the World
Charlotte Perkins	Yellow Wallpaper (not in anthology)
John Barth	Life-Story

3. Minimalism

Amy Hempel	In the Cemetery Where Al Jolson Is Buried
Ann Beattie	The Burning House

4. Satire

Ursula Le Guin	The New Atlantis
Tom Robbins	The Chink and the Clock People

5. Perspective Is All

William Trevor	Beyond the Pale
Ernest Gaines	Just Like a Tree
Robert Coover	The Babysitter
Joyce Carol Oates	How I Contemplated the World from the Detroit House of Correction and Began My Life Over Again

6. Life and Art; Art and Life
   Alice Walker   Everyday Use

II "Writing about Literature"   **Teacher: Janet Missavage**
Course Readings:
1. Fiction is a mirror.
   Alice Munro   Boys and Girls (not in anthol-
                                     ogy)
   Alice Adams   Barcelona
   Raymond Carver   Where I'm Calling From
   Beth Nugent   City of Boys
2. The mirror looks back at itself.
   John Barth   Life-Story
   Woody Allen   The Kugelmass Episode
   Woody Allen   The Purple Rose of Cairo
                                     (movie)
   Donald Barthelme   The Indian Uprising
3. The mirror is fractured.
   Margaret Atwood   Rape Fantasies
   Robert Coover   The Babysitter
   Total Recall (movie)
   Rashomon (movie)
   William Trevor   Beyond the Pale

ISSUES FOR DISCUSSION

• What similarities do you see between these two conceptions of the "Writing about Literature" course, as suggested by the reading lists and the unit titles? Dan thinks Janet's unit titles are more promising than Larry's—and not only because he likes metaphors. Do you agree? When Larry taught his course a second time, he changed the titles of units 3 and 4, "Minimalism" and "Satire," to "Realism" and "Fantasy." Does the title change appear to strengthen coherence in his sequence?

• Could you construct one or two general questions that would be more relevant for each unit in Janet's and Larry's sequences? Would questions focus on the readers? authors? texts? Would the focus change within a unit or from one unit to the next?

• Both Janet and Larry began with stories not in their anthology— stories chosen in order to make possible certain kinds of early, informal writing assignments. Larry started with the very brief Katharine Brush story, "Birthday Party," and asked his students to write what they thought happened next, that is, after the story ended. Janet distributed the first few paragraphs of Alice Munro's "Boys and Girls," in which it is not possible to tell for certain whether the narrator is a boy or a girl. She asked her students to finish the story as credibly as they could, given the opening. Then she distributed the rest of Munro's story in which the identity of the narrator is revealed. In what ways are these assignments similar? What values do you think Janet and Larry hoped to achieve by making the assignments? Are they likely to have succeeded? Do you think one assignment is more promising than the other?

Another teacher gave an opening assignment that did not involve a literary text: he asked the students to write a brief history of their own experience as readers and writers—what writing specialist Wendy Bishop calls a "literacy autobiography." How would the values implicit in this assignment compare with those sought by Larry and Janet? How might students' written responses to these various opening assignments be used in the classroom?

• As noted above, Janet used movies along with short stories in her course. With the stories that might be called self-reflexive fictions, she showed Woody Allen's *The Purple Rose of Cairo,* and with the stories where the point of view shifts surprisingly, she showed *Total Recall* and *Rashomon.* Dan asked her whether she would do this again, and she said, "Absolutely. The flicks helped the students read the stories, and the stories helped them read the flicks." But when Dan talked with Charlie, who taught a poetry-based version of the "Writing about Literature" course, he got a different response entirely. Charlie showed D. W. Griffiths's *The New York Hat* during the first week of his course. His rationale was as follows:

> Silent cinema has been likened to poetry, and opposed to the supposed purpose of talkies: the organization is by image, and narrative tends to be more implied than explicated. A visual text may be read as readily as a verbal; this assignment can be connected with that of having the students draw a poem. The text will be both strange to the students, many of whom will never have seen any silent film before, and familiar as a story in pictures on a screen. The watching will be an opportunity to relate ideas of reading a text, which they may associate only with schoolbooks, to an alternative medium; they will be at once distanced from and approximated to the customary. I'm hoping they'll be able to make the leap.

They weren't—or at least they didn't. The students were mildly amused by the Griffiths film, but they ignored Charlie's efforts to relate it to the reading of poetry. Why do you think using film together with printed texts might have worked well in one case, but not in the other?

• In *Textual Power*, Robert Scholes discusses three kinds of activities that students need to undertake: reading, that is, constructing texts; interpreting, that is, identifying in thematic terms what texts are about; and criticizing, that is, evaluating the world views that texts imply. On the last, he suggests that students should "at some level, in some way... be invited into ... critical debates." Do you think the writing of critics has a place in a "Writing about Literature" course? If so, why, when, and how would you introduce it?

• As you will recall, the composition advisory committee thinks the range of readings for "Writing about Literature" should be deliberately limited. Do you agree? If so, is genre choice a good approach? What are the pros and cons of limiting reading selections by genre? by time period? by author? by theme? by some combination?

• If genre is chosen as a way to limit, what would be the advantages of working with short fiction? with poetry? with drama? What special reading difficulties and writing assignment opportunities would come with each choice? Would larger issues relevant to writing about literature be more readily raised with one genre than with another?

• The composition advisory committee may change the anthology for the fiction sections of "Writing about Literature," replacing *The Norton Anthology of Contemporary Fiction* (Cassill) with *The Story and Its Writer* (Charters) from Bedford Books. Would you prefer the Bedford collection, which limits readings by genre only, or the Norton, which limits by both genre and time? What are the advantages and disadvantages of dealing only with contemporary work in a "Writing about Literature" course? How should a genre-limited "Writing about Literature" course be different from an "Introduction to Fiction" (or Poetry or Drama)?

The Bedford collection contains about one hundred stories, more than twice the number in the Norton book. Students were assigned only about fifteen stories in the course at Dan's school. Should the size of a collection be considered in making a choice?

• Do you think it is appropriate for a writing-and-literature course to satisfy a university's composition requirement? What kind of relation should students be encouraged to see between writing in such a course and writing in other English courses or in other disciplines?

Note

1. The writing assignment sequence is taken from *Purposes and Ideas: Readings for University Writing*, edited by David A. Jolliffe (Dubuque, Iowa: Kendall Hunt, 1991), 385–89. Reprinted by permission of Kendall Hunt.

Works Cited

Adams, Alice. 1988. "Barcelona." In Cassill, *The Norton Anthology of Contemporary Fiction*, 7–10.

Allen, Woody. 1988. "The Kugelmass Episode." In Cassill, *The Notron Anthology of Contemporary Fiction*, 11–19.

Atwood, Margaret. 1988. "Rape Fantasies." In Cassill, *The Norton Anthology of Contemporary Fiction*, 19–27.

Barth, John. 1988. "Life-Story." In Cassill, *The Norton Anthology of Contemporary Fiction*, 27–37.

Barthelme, Donald. 1988. "The Indian Uprising." In Cassill, *The Norton Anthology of Contemporary Fiction*, 37–42.

Barthes, Roland. 1979. "The Men in the Street on Strike." In *The Eiffel Tower and Other Mythologies*, translated by Richard Howard, 99–102. New York: Hill and Wang.

Beattie, Ann. 1988. "The Burning House." In Cassill, *The Norton Anthology of Contemporary Fiction*, 42–55.

Bellah, Robert N., Richard Madsen, William M. Sullivan, Ann Swidler, and Steven M. Tipton. 1985. *Habits of the Heart: Individualism and Commitment in American Life.* Berkeley: University of California Press.

Belsey, Catherine. 1980. "Criticism and Meaning." In *Critical Practice*, 37–55. London and New York: Methuen.

Berger, John. 1990. "Ways of Seeing." In *Ways of Reading: An Anthology for Writers*, 2nd ed., edited by David Bartholomae and Anthony Petrosky, 65–92. Boston: Bedford Books of St. Martin's.

Bly, Carol. 1990. "Growing Up Expressive." In Smart, *Eight Modern Essayists*, 201–8.

Brecht, Bertolt. 1947. "The Worker Reads History." In *Bertolt Brecht: Selected Poems*, translated by H. R. Hays. New York: Grove.

Carver, Raymond. 1988. "Where I'm Calling From." In Cassill, *The Norton Anthology of Contemporary Fiction*, 64–77.

Cassill, R. V., ed. 1988. *The Norton Anthology of Contemporary Fiction.* New York: W. W. Norton.

———, ed. 1990. *The Norton Anthology of Short Fiction.* New York: W. W. Norton.

Cesaire, Aime. 1972. *Discourse on Colonialism*, translated by Joan Pinkham. New York: Monthly Review Press.

Charters, Ann. 1991. *The Story and Its Writer: An Introduction to Short Fiction*, 3rd ed. Boston: Bedford Books.

Coles, William F., Jr. 1974. *Teaching Composition.* Upper Montclair, N.J.: Boynton-Cook.

Consumers Union. 1986. "It's Natural! It's Organic! Or Is It?" In *Language Awareness,* 4th ed., edited by Paul Eschholz, Alfred Rosa, and Virginia Clark, 229–38. New York: St. Martin's Press.

Coover, Robert. 1988. "The Babysitter." In Cassill, *The Norton Anthology of Contemporary Fiction,* 78–99.

Cox, Murray. 1990. "Paulo Freire (Interview)." *Omni* 12(7): 74, 78, 79, 94.

Crews, Frederick. 1980. *The Random House Handbook,* 3rd ed. New York: Random House.

Didion, Joan. 1979. "At the Dam." In *The White Album,* 198–201. New York: Simon and Schuster.

Dowdey, Diane. 1990. *The Researching Reader: Source-Based Writings across the Disciplines.* Fort Worth, Tex.: Holt, Rinehart & Winston.

D'Souza, Dinesh. 1991. *Illiberal Education.* New York: Free Press.

Eagleton, Terry. 1976. "The Author as Producer." In *Marxism and Literary Criticism,* 59–76. Berkeley and Los Angeles: University of California Press.

Ehrenreich, Barbara. 1991. "Farewell to Work." In Jolliffe, *Purposes and Ideas.*

———. 1989. *Fear of Falling: The Inner Life of the Middle Class.* New York: Pantheon Books.

Fasteau, Marc Feigen. 1991. "Friendships Among Men." In Jolliffe, *Purposes and Ideas.*

Fussell, Paul. 1990. "Appearance Counts." In Smart, *Eight Modern Essayists,* 138–59.

Gaines, Ernest. 1988. "Just Like a Tree." In Cassill, *The Norton Anthology of Contemporary Fiction,* 155–73.

Guillen, Nicolas. 1987. "Poem of Underdevelopment." Quoted in *Resistance Literature,* by Barbara Harlow, 31–32. New York and London: Methuen.

Guillen, Tomas. 1986. "What to Call an American of Hispanic Descent." In *Language Awareness,* 4th ed., edited by Paul Eschholz, Alfred Rosa, and Virginia Clark, 281–5. New York: St. Martin's Press.

Gussow, Mel. 1988, July 3. "From the City Streets, A Poet of the Stage." *The New York Times,* 8H.

Harlow, Barbara. 1987. "Prison Memoirs of Political Detainees." In *Resistance Literature,* 117–53. New York and London: Methuen.

Hempel, Amy. 1988. "In the Cemetery Where Al Jolson Is Buried." In Cassill, *The Norton Anthology of Contemporary Fiction,* 249–56.

Hook, Sidney. 1991. "In Defense of Voluntary Euthanasia." In *Conversations,* edited by Jack Selzer. New York: Macmillan.

Hooks, Bell. 1986, Nov. "Coming to Voice." *Zeta Magazine,* 45–49.

Howard, Jane. 1991. "Families." In *Prose in Brief: Reading and Writing Essays,* edited by Edward Proffitt, 315–20. San Diego: Harcourt Brace Jovanovich.

Hughes, Langston. 1991. "Salvation." In *Outlooks and Insights: A Reader for College Writers,* 3rd ed., edited by Paul Eschholz and Alfred Rosa, 85–87. New York: St. Martin's Press.

John Paul II. 1991. "On Human Work." In Jolliffe, *Purposes and Ideas.*

Jolliffe, David A., ed. 1991. *Purposes and Ideas: Readings for University Writing,* 2nd ed. Dubuque, Iowa: Kendall Hunt.

Kazin, Alfred. 1979. "The Kitchen." In *A Walker in the City.* San Diego: Harcourt Brace Jovanovich.

Kennedy, Mary Lynch, William J. Kennedy, and Hadley M. Smith. 1987. *Writing in the Disciplines: A Reader for Writers.* Englewood Cliffs, N.J.: Prentice-Hall.

King, Martin Luther, Jr. 1991. "Letter from Birmingham Jail." In Jolliffe, *Purposes and Ideas.*

Kiniry, Malcolm, and Mike Rose, eds. 1990. *Critical Strategies for Academic Writing: Cases, Assignments, and Readings.* Boston: Bedford Books.

Kinneavy, James. 1971. *A Theory of Discourse.* New York: Norton.

Lakoff, Robin. 1986. "You Are What You Say." In *Language Awareness,* 4th ed., edited by Paul Eschholz, Alfred Rosa, and Virginia Clark, 311–18. New York: St. Martin's Press.

Lanham, Richard A. 1979. *Revising Prose.* New York: Scribners.

Le Guin, Ursula K. 1988. "The New Atlantis." In Cassill, *The Norton Anthology of Contemporary Fiction,* 270–90.

Leo, John. 1988, Aug. "Take Me, Hurt Me, Smoke Me: An Advertising Case Study." *Spy Magazine,* 106–9.

MacIntyre, Alasdair G. 1984. *After Virtue: A Study in Moral Theory,* 2nd ed. Notre Dame, Ind.: University of Notre Dame Press.

Malcolm X. 1990. From *The Autobiography of Malcolm X.* In Kiniry and Rose, *Critical Strategies for Academic Writing.*

———. 1986. "Coming to an Awareness of Language." In *Language Awareness,* 4th ed., edited by Paul Eschholz, Alfred Rosa, and Virginia Clark, 13–16. New York: St. Martin's Press.

Marquez, Gabriel Garcia. 1988. "The Handsomest Drowned Man in the World." In Cassill, *The Norton Anthology of Contemporary Fiction,* 197–201.

McCullers, Carson. 1991. "Loneliness: An American Malady." In Jolliffe, *Purposes and Ideas.*

McKay, Claude. 1969. "If We Must Die." In *Selected Poems.* San Diego: Harcourt Brace Jovanovich.

Mead, Margaret. 1991. "Rage, Rhythm, and Autonomy." In Jolliffe, *Purposes and Ideas.*

Moffett, James. 1968. *Teaching the Universe of Discourse.* New York: Houghton Mifflin.

Moore, Joan. 1990. From *Homeboys: Gangs, Drugs, and Prison in the Barrios of Los Angeles.* In Kiniry and Rose, *Critical Strategies for Academic Writing.*

Munro, Alice. 1985. "Boys and Girls." In *The Norton Introduction to Fiction,* 3rd ed., edited by Jerome Beaty, 339–50. New York: W. W. Norton.

Nugent, Beth. 1988. "City of Boys." In Cassill, *The Norton Anthology of Contemporary Fiction,* 343–54.

Oates, Joyce Carol. 1988. "How I Contemplated the World from the Detroit House of Correction and Began My Life over Again." In Cassill, *The Norton Anthology of Contemporary Fiction,* 355–67.

Orwell, George. 1961. "Why Do I Write?" in *A Collection of Essays,* 309–16. London: Secker.

Plato. 1991. "Crito." In Jolliffe, *Purposes and Ideas.*

Rachels, James. 1986. *The Elements of Moral Philosophy.* Philadelphia: Temple University Press.

Rich, Adrienne. 1990. "When We Dead Re-Awaken: Writing as Re-Vision." In *Ways of Reading: An Anthology for Writers,* 2nd ed., edited by David Bartholomae and Anthony Petrosky, 480–98. Boston: Bedford Books of St. Martin's.

Ringle, Ken. 1990, Sept. 7. "Ellis Island: The Half-Opened Door." *Washington Post,* style section, 1.

Robbins, Tom. 1988. "The Chink and the Clock People." In Cassill, *The Norton Anthology of Contemporary Fiction,* 410–23.

Rodriguez, Richard. 1991. "Aria: A Memoir of a Bilingual Childhood." In Jolliffe, *Purposes and Ideas.*

Sarton, May. 1991. "The Rewards of Living a Solitary Life." In Jolliffe, *Purposes and Ideas.*

Scholes, Robert. 1985. *Textual Power: Literary Theory and the Teaching of English.* New Haven, Conn.: Yale University Press.

Seiter, Ellen. 1987. "Semiotics and Television." In *Channels of Discourse: Television and Contemporary Criticism,* edited by Robert C. Allen, 17–41. Chapel Hill and London: University of North Carolina Press.

Sizer, Theodore. 1984. "What High School Is." In *Horace's Compromise.* New York: Houghton Mifflin.

Smart, William, ed. 1990. *Eight Modern Essayists.* New York: St. Martin's Press.

Smith, Huston. 1991. "The Hindu Way to God through Work." In Jolliffe, *Purposes and Ideas.*

Syfers, Judy. 1971, Dec. 31. "I Want a Wife." *Ms.*

Terkel, Studs. 1974. *Working.* New York: Avon.

Thoreau, Henry David. 1960. "Brute Neighbors." *Walden,* edited by Sherman Paul. Boston: Houghton Mifflin

Tompkins, Jane. 1990. "At the Buffalo Bill Museum—June 1988." *South Atlantic Quarterly,* 89(3): 525–45.

Trevor, William. 1988. "Beyond the Pale." In Cassill, *The Norton Anthology of Contemporary Fiction,* 459–80.

Truth, Sojourner. 1991. "Ain't I a Woman?" In *Conversations,* edited by Jack Selzer. New York: Macmillan.

Walker, Alice. 1990. "The Civil Rights Movement: What Good Was It?" In Smart, *Eight Modern Essayists,* 249–55.

———. 1973. "Everyday Use." In *Love and Trouble.* San Diego: Harcourt Brace Jovanovich.

White, E. B. 1990. "Death of a Pig." In Smart, *Eight Modern Essayists,* 86–94.

———. 1990. "On a Florida Key." In Smart, *Eight Modern Essayists,* 98–103.

———. 1990. "Once More to the Lake." In Smart, *Eight Modern Essayists,* 80–86.

Woolf, Virginia. 1991. From *A Room of One's Own.* In Jolliffe, *Purposes and Ideas.*

A Bibliography
of Professional Sources

In the following bibliography, we present some useful works for teachers of writing in college and university settings. The list begins with general works on the teaching of writing, most of which focus in varying degrees on the subjects of the six chapters in *Scenarios for Teaching Writing*. For more specific treatments, we have also included references to books and journal articles to accompany each chapter. This list is, of course, intended only as a starting point for further explorations into the theory and practice of writing instruction.

Books on the Teaching of Writing

Camp, G., ed. 1982. *Teaching Writing: Essays from the Bay Area Writing Project.* Upper Montclair, N.J.: Boynton/Cook.

Coles, W. E., Jr. 1974. *Teaching Composition.* Upper Montclair, N.J.: Boynton/Cook.

———. 1978. *The Plural I: The Teaching of Writing.* New York: Holt, Rinehart & Winston.

Deen, R., and M. Ponsot. 1982. *Beat Not the Poor Desk: Writing: What to Teach, How to Teach It, and Why.* Upper Montclair, N.J.: Boynton/Cook.

Fulwiler, T. 1987. *Teaching with Writing.* Portsmouth, N.H.: Heinemann-Boynton/Cook.

Irmscher, W. F. 1979. *Teaching Expository Writing.* New York: Holt, Rinehart & Winston.

Judy, S. N., and S. J. Judy. 1981. *An Introduction to the Teaching of Writing.* New York: Wiley.

Koch, C., and J. M. Brazil. 1981. *Strategies for Teaching the Composing Process.* Urbana, Ill.: National Council of Teachers of English.

Lindemann, E. 1987. *A Rhetoric for Writing Teachers,* 2nd ed. New York: Oxford.

McQuade, D. 1979. *Linguistics, Stylistics, and the Teaching of Composition.* Akron, Ohio: University of Akron/L&S Books.

Moffett, J. 1968. *Teaching the Universe of Discourse.* Boston: Houghton Mifflin.

Murray, D. 1982. *Learning by Teaching: Selected Articles on Writing and Teaching.* Upper Montclair, N.J.: Boynton/Cook.

———. 1985. *A Writer Teaches Writing,* 2nd ed. Boston: Houghton Mifflin.

Myers, M., and J. Gray, eds. 1983. *Theory and Practice in the Teaching of Composition.* Urbana, Ill.: National Council of Teachers of English.

Neman, B. 1980. *Teaching Students to Write.* Columbus, Ohio: Merrill.

Tate, G., and E. P. J. Corbett. 1967. *Teaching Freshman Composition.* New York: Oxford.

———. 1976. *Teaching Composition: Ten Bibliographic Essays.* Fort Worth, Tex.: Texas Christian University Press.

———, eds. 1981. *The Writing Teacher's Sourcebook.* New York: Oxford.

Chapter 1: Creating Effective Writing Assignments

Bartholomae, D. 1983. "Writing Assignments: Where Writing Begins." In *Fforum: Essays on Theory and Practice in the Teaching of Writing,* edited by P. Stock, 300–12. Upper Montclair, N.J.: Boynton/Cook.

Coles, W. E., Jr. 1970. "The Sense of Nonsense as a Design for Sequential Writing Assignments." *College Composition and Communication* 21:27–34.

Hillocks, G., Jr. 1986. *Research on Written Composition: New Directions for Teaching.* Urbana, Ill.: National Conference on Research in English; ERIC Clearinghouse on Reading and Communication Skills.

Lees, E. O. 1979. *Respecting the Learner's Expertise: Assignments that Ask Students to Write about Composing.* Bloomington, Ind.: ERIC Clearinghouse on Reading and Communication Skills. ERIC Document Reproduction Service No. ED 184 129.

Lunsford, A. 1986. "Assignments for Basic Writers: Unresolved Issues and Needed Research." *Journal of Basic Writing* 5:87–99.

MacDonald, S. P. 1987. "Problem Definition in Academic Writing." *College English* 49(3):315–31.

Chapter 2: Using Readings in Writing Courses

Corcoran, W., and E. Evans, eds. 1987. *Readers, Texts, Teachers.* Upper Montclair, N.J.: Boynton/Cook.

Fish, S. 1980. *Is There a Text in This Class? The Authority of Interpretive Communities.* Cambridge, Mass.: Harvard University Press.

Gould, C., and K. Gould. 1986. "College Anthologies of Readings and Assumptions about Literacy." *College Composition and Communication* 37:204–11.

Hayhoe, M., and S. Parker, eds. 1990. *Reading and Response.* Philadelphia and Buckingham,U.K.: Milton Keynes and Open University Press.

Nelms, B. F., ed. 1988. *Literature in the Classroom: Readers, Texts, and Contexts.* Urbana, Ill.: National Council of Teachers of English.

Newkirk, T. 1986. *Only Connect: Uniting Writing and Reading.* Upper Montclair, N.J.: Boynton/Cook.

Nist, S., and D. L. Mealey. 1991. "Teacher-Directed Comprehension Strategies." In *Teaching Reading and Study Strategies at the College Level,* edited by R. F. Flippo and D. C. Caverly, 42–85. Newark, Del.: International Reading Association.

Salvatori, M. 1983. "Reading and Writing a Text: Correlations between Reading and Writing Patterns." *College English* 45(7):657–66.

Scholes, R. 1985. *Textual Power: Literary Theory and the Teaching of English.* New Haven, Conn.: Yale University Press.

Tierney, R. J., P. L. Anders, and J. N. Mitchell, eds. 1987. *Understanding Readers' Understanding: Theory and Practice.* Hillsdale, N.J.: Lawrence Erlbaum.

Trimbur, J. 1984. "Literature and Composition: Separatism or Convergence?" *Journal of Teaching Writing* 3(1):109–15.

Chapter 3: Responding to Student Writing

Anson, C. M. 1982. "The Artificial Art of Evaluating Writing." *Journal of Teaching Writing* 1(2):159–70.

———, ed. 1989. *Writing and Response: Theory, Practice and Research.* Urbana, Ill.: National Council of Teachers of English.

Berkenkotter, C. 1984. "Student Writers and Their Sense of Authority over Texts." *College Composition and Communication* 35(3):312–19.

Brannon, L., and C. H. Knoblauch. 1982. "On Students' Right to Their Own Texts: A Model of Teacher Response." *College Composition and Communication* 33(2):157–66.

Cooper, C. R., and L. Odell, eds. 1977. *Evaluating Writing: Describing, Measuring, Judging.* Urbana, Ill.: National Council of Teachers of English.

Lawson, B., S. Sterr Ryan, and W. R. Winterowd, eds. 1989. *Encountering Student Texts: Interpretive Issues in Reading Student Writing.* Urbana, Ill.: National Council of Teachers of English.

Sommers, N. 1982. "Responding to Student Writing." *College Composition and Communication* 33:148–87.

Spear, K. 1988. *Sharing Writing: Peer Response Groups in English Classes.* Portsmouth, N.H.: Boynton/Cook.

White, E. M. 1984. "Post-Structural Literary Criticism and the Response to Student Writing." *College Composition and Communication* 35(2):186–95.

Chapter 4: Teaching "Grammar," Usage, and Style in Context

Bartholomae, D. 1980. "The Study of Error." *College Composition and Communication* 31:253–69.

Haswell, R. H. 1988. "Error and Change in College Student Writing." *Written Communication* 5(9):479–99.

Kolln, M. 1990. *Understanding English Grammar,* 3rd ed. New York: Macmillan.

———. 1991. *Rhetorical Grammar.* New York: Macmillan.

MacDonald, S. P. 1986. "Specificity in Context: Some Difficulties for the Inexperienced Writer." *College Composition and Communication* 37(2):195–203.

Shaughnessy, M. 1977. *Errors and Expectations.* New York: Oxford University Press.

Wall, S. V., and G. A. Hull. 1989. "The Semantics of Error: What Do Teachers Know?" In *Writing and Response,* edited by C. M. Anson, 261–92. Urbana, Ill.: National Council of Teachers of English.

Williams, J. 1981. "The Phenomenology of Error." *College Composition and Communication* 32(2):152–68.

Chapter 5: Managing Discourse in Classes, Conferences, and Small Groups

Beach, R. 1989. "Showing Students How to Assess: Demonstrating Techniques for Response in the Writing Conference." In *Writing and Response,* edited by C. M. Anson, 127–48. Urbana, Ill.: National Council of Teachers of English.

Brooke, R. E. 1991. *Writing and Sense of Self: Identity Negotiation in Writing Workshops.* Urbana, Ill.: National Council of Teachers of English.

Bruffee, K. A. 1983. "Writing and Reading as Collaborative or Social Acts." In *The Writer's Mind,* edited by J. N. Hayes, P. A. Roth, J. R. Ramsey, and R. D. Foulke, 159–70. Urbana, Ill.: National Council of Teachers of English.

———. 1984. "Collaborative Learning and the 'Conversation of Mankind'." *College English* 46(7)635–52.

Carnicelli, T. 1980. "The Writing Conference: A One-to-One Conversation." In *Eight Approaches to Teaching Composition,* edited by T. R. Donovan and B. W. McClelland, 101–31. Urbana, Ill.: National Council of Teachers of English.

Freedman, S. W., ed. 1985. *The Acquisition of Written Language: Response and Revision.* New York: Ablex.

George, D. 1984. "Working with Peer Groups in the Composition Classroom." *College Composition and Communication* 35(3):320–26.

Gere, A. R. 1987. *Writing Groups: History, Theory, and Implications.* Carbondale, Ill.: Southern Illinois University Press.

Harris, M. 1986. *Teaching One-to-One: The Writing Conference.* Urbana, Ill.: National Council of Teachers of English.

Jacobs, S. E., and A. Karlinger. 1977. "Helping Students to Think: The Effect of Speech Roles in Individual Conferences on Quality of Thought in Student Writing." *College English* 38(5):489–505.

Newkirk, T. 1984. "Direction and Misdirection in Peer Response." *College Composition and Communication* 35(3):300–11.

———. 1984. "How Students Read Student Papers: An Exploratory Study." *Written Communication* 1(3):283–305.

———. 1989. "The First Five Minutes: Setting the Agenda in a Writing Conference." In *Writing and Response,* edited by C. M. Anson, 317–31. Urbana, Ill.: National Council of Teachers of English.

Nystrand, M., and D. Brandt. 1989. "Response to Writing as a Context for Learning to Write." In *Writing and Response,* edited by C. M. Anson, 209–30. Urbana, Ill.: National Council of Teachers of English.

Thomas, D., and G. Thomas. 1989. "The Use of Rogerian Reflection in Small-Group Writing Conferences." In *Writing and Response,* edited by C. M. Anson, 114–26. Urbana, Ill.: National Council of Teachers of English.

Trimbur, J. 1989. "Consensus and Difference in Collaborative Learning." *College English* 51(6):602–16.

Chapter 6: Teaching Writing: Course Designs

Bartholomae, D., and A. Petrosky. 1986. *Facts, Artifacts and Counterfacts: Theory and Method for a Reading and Writing Course.* Upper Montclair, N.J.: Boynton/Cook.

Bishop, W. 1986. "Texts and Contexts: A Social-Rhetorical Model for Teaching Writing-with-Literature Courses." *The Writing Instructor,* Summer: 190–202.

Carden, P. 1984. "Designing a Course." In *Teaching Prose: A Guide for Writing Instructors,* edited by F. V. Bogel and K. K. Gottschalk, 20–45. New York: W. W. Norton.

Connolly, P., and T. Vilardi, eds. 1986. *New Methods in College Writing Programs.* New York: Modern Language Association.

Donovan, T. R., and B. W. McClelland, eds. 1980. *Eight Approaches to Teaching Composition.* Urbana, Ill.: National Council of Teachers of English.

Kail, H. 1988. "Narratives of Knowledge: Story and Pedagogy in Four Composition Texts." *Rhetoric Review* 6(2):179–91.

Klaus, C. M., and N. Jones, eds. 1984. *Courses for Change in Writing: A Selection from the NEH/Iowa Institute.* Upper Montclair, N.J.: Boynton/Cook.

Rose, M. 1983. "Remedial Writing Courses: A Critique and a Proposal." *College English* 45(2):109–28.

Sherman, S. W. 1986. "Inventing an Elephant: History as Composition." In *Only Connect: Uniting Reading and Writing,* edited by T. Newkirk, 211–26. Upper Montclair, N.J.: Boynton/Cook.

Welch, K. 1987. "Ideology and Freshman Textbook Production: The Place of Theory in Writing Pedagogy." *College Composition and Communication* 38(3):269–82.

Authors

Chris M. Anson is associate professor of English and director of composition at the University of Minnesota, where he supervises more than one hundred instructors and teaches graduate courses in writing theory and research. He has published six books on composition, among them an NCTE collection, *Writing and Response: Theory, Practice and Research.* His articles and chapters have appeared in numerous journals and collections of essays. His research interests include writing across the curriculum (with special emphasis on writing to learn), response to writing, and the nature of literacy in and out of schools.

Joan Graham directs the University of Washington's Interdisciplinary Writing Program, which offers writing courses linked with lecture courses in disciplines across the curriculum. Because of her interest in the effects of writers' contexts, the roles of writing in learning, and the problems of writing course design, she has become increasingly involved in the training of teaching assistants. She has also served as a consultant on the uses of writing in teaching at schools around the country. Currently, she is codirecting a large, longitudinal study of students' writing experience at the University of Washington.

David A. Jolliffe is director of English composition and chair of the Writing-in-the-Disciplines Board, University of Illinois at Chicago (UIC). He is coauthor of *Assessing Writers' Knowledge and Processes of Composing,* contributing editor of *Writing in Academic Disciplines,* editor of *Purposes and Ideas: Readings for University Writing,* and author of *Writing in and for the Disciplines.* He supervises ninety instructors who teach composition to 6,000 students a year. He oversees a writing-in-the-disciplines program for twenty-five departments in UIC's College of Liberal Arts and Sciences.

Nancy S. Shapiro has had extensive experience as a writing program administrator at the University of Maryland, which has one of the leading writing programs in the country. She teaches courses in writing theory and pedagogy, advanced composition, technical writing, editing and document design, and freshman composition. Her essays and reviews appear in *College Composition and Communication, Literary Research,* and *Virginia State Reading Association Journal.* Her current research centers on student and teacher growth in the writing classroom. She and Chris Anson cochair the Writing Group of the Alliance for Undergraduate Education.

Carolyn H. Smith is director of freshman English at the University of Florida, where she provides teaching assistants with a training workshop and a semester-long course on current theories about writing and teaching. She has participated in the Florida Writing Project and presented papers on her current research project, Josephine Miles and other pioneer women in composition.